Easy Piano Book for Beginners

Start from The Basics and Teach Yourself to Play Famous Piano Songs, Read Music and Learn The Best Techniques to Become An Excellent Pianist

Angela Ferrante

Contents

Introduction

Even if you have no prior musical training, Easy Piano Book for Beginners is a compilation of well-known songs that you can play straight away. Simple charts that show you where to place your fingers and how to interpret the music are used to arrange songs from simplest to toughest. Begin slowly and develop your talents. Find out about a wide range of popular tunes, including classics and well-known music. This book helps you save time by outlining just what you need to do to get going right away. Play your preferred music right away! With large print, evenly spaced sheet music that is simple to read, you may master your favorite tunes while learning the fundamentals of piano technique. This song collection was thoughtfully chosen by a top piano instructor. Each item is enjoyable and simple to use. Even if you have no idea where to begin, then this wholesome Piano guide will help you learn about the notes, the chords, and all the scales that are used to play the songs.

Getting Started

Whether they are novices or professionals, pianists should constantly strive to improve. Whether you've taken piano lessons before or are just beginning, progress and improvement are essential. Here are a few ways you might develop as a pianist, from strengthening your fingers to always pushing yourself.

Manage Your Practice Time

Do you only practice during your free time? You might not have noticed much improvement as a result of this. It shouldn't be low on your list of priorities to practice the piano. You should set aside some time each week to sit down and practice your instrument, even if it's at the bottom of the list. Find a schedule and stick to it, whether you practice for 30 minutes every Monday, Wednesday, and Friday or for an hour every day of the week. Finding the appropriate teacher is crucial, but so is your dedication to practicing. Add an additional hour of practice time to your schedule if you do have some extra time.

Practice Sight Reading

It's a good idea to sit down and practice one piece of music until you can play it flawlessly, but every so often, vary things up by adding a random piece. Don't worry too much about making mistakes when you're practicing your sight reading. Play the piece as best you can from beginning to end, and then repeat it a couple more times for accuracy. Sight reading is a talent that is necessary for everyone who wants to join a band or orchestra, and it also improves improvisation skills. When you do make mistakes, try not to let them depress or weigh you down. If you believe that making mistakes is an essential component of learning, you'll probably

Slow Down

Does the speed at which a piece is played reveal a musician's true ability? While this may be true in some situations, playing too quickly can cause one to miss notes and play sloppily. Avoid playing a portion too rapidly if you find yourself missing notes in it; instead, pause the metronome, play it slowly, and practice it until you get it correctly. No matter how well you believe you know a piece, every three or four runs through, practice it more slowly. After all, how can you ever expect to play a piece swiftly if you can't perform it at a slower tempo?

Keep Challenging Yourself

Although it may seem obvious, you'd be shocked at how many pianists stop pushing themselves once they reach a certain level of proficiency. Just like with any skill, you have to push yourself to get better. Ask your instructor for advice if you're unsure about which song to choose for your challenge. They will be able to choose a piece that is difficult but manageable because they will know your skills and weaknesses better than anyone. They should be able to choose a piece that focuses mostly on the left hand, for instance, if you have trouble playing with their left hand.

Make Sure Your Goals are Realistic

Make sure the goals you're setting are reasonable, regardless of what they are. Don't expect to learn how to play the piano brilliantly overnight. Any instrument may be improved with practice, commitment, and effort. We're simply human, and as humans, we often have lofty aspirations. Consider re-evaluating your goals if you're having trouble achieving them. Make a list, then discuss it with your piano instructor. Based on your present skill set, they will be able to tell whether your ambitions are doable or excessively ambitious.

Play Classical Music Pieces

Listen to us if you believe that classical music is monotonous. Technically speaking, classical music can be difficult. Your technical skills will start to advance as you begin working with some of the more challenging parts. Not only will classical music provide you with a strong foundation, but it will also push you to grow as a musician. Bach and Chopin are fantastic places to start if you've never played classical music before. Select challenging pieces because if you simply play repertoire you are already familiar with, you won't advance.

Playing in Public Practice

You should become accustomed to playing the piano in front of people as a pianist. Put on a rehearsal for your friends and family to get yourself ready for the gig. Feeling at ease when performing is essential, whether you are playing for one person or 100. Invite some cousins or friends around for a recital after you feel at ease performing for your parents. Start off by playing at private gatherings like Christmas parties, picnics, or school activities. One day, doing a performance in front of an audience won't be a huge issue, and your sweaty hands will be a thing of the past.

Discovering Music

Over the past 600 years, the majority of classical music's most well-known composers have followed Western cultural traditions. Determining which of these composers is the most important sparks the hottest argument among classical music academics and fans. They varied in style, skill, invention, and popularity. Beethoven, Bach, and Mozart are the three composers who constantly rank first. On the rest, academics and fans have different opinions, although the ones below are frequently thought to be some of the most important.

Beethoven

Most people agree that Ludwig van Beethoven, a German musician, and composer, is the greatest composer to have ever lived. He broadened the classical traditions of Wolfgang Amadeus Mozart and Joseph Haydn, two of his instructors, and experimented with personal expression, a quality that had an impact on the Romantic composers who came after him. Although he suffered from gradual deafness throughout his life and career, the illness did not stop him from creating some of his most significant works in the last ten years of his life when he was almost completely deaf. Beethoven's significant compositions span the sonata, symphony, concerto, and quartet genres. These include Moonlight Sonata, Für Elise, Symphony 9 in D Minor, and Op. 125, and Symphony 5 in C Minor, Op. 67.

Bach

German composer and organist Johann Sebastian Bach lived throughout the Baroque era. While his contemporaries appreciated him for his musical abilities, they considered his compositions were out of date. Early in the 19th century, his work was rediscovered, and this sparked the so-called Bach revival, which elevated him to the status of one of the greatest composers ever. The Well-Tempered Clavier, Brandenburg Concertos, Suites for Unaccompanied Cello, Orchestral Suites, Mass in B Minor, BWV 232, and The Well-Tempered Clavier are some of his most well-known works.

Mozart

Wolfgang Amadeus Mozart, an Austrian Classical composer, is known as one of the finest composers of Western music. He is the only composer who has created works that are outstanding in every musical genre of the time. Mozart started his career as a child prodigy, rumored to have the capacity to play music at age three and create music at age five. The Marriage of Figaro, Madigan, and Clarinet in A Major, K 581 are notable works.

Brahms

German pianist and composer Johannes Brahms belonged to the Romantic era, yet he was more of a Classical school follower. He composed music in a variety of styles, including choral compositions, chamber music, piano works, symphonies, concerti, and concertos, many of which show the influence of folk music. His best-known compositions include Hungarian Dances, Wiegenlied, and Op. 49, No. 4, and Symphony No. 3 in F Major.

Wagner

Richard Wagner, a German composer and thinker revolutionized Western music while extending the operatic tradition. His use of leitmotifs, or brief melodic themes for a person, place, or thing, which he expertly transformed throughout a work, is particularly well recognized for his dramatic compositions. His operas Tannhäuser, Lohengrin, Tristan, The Flying Dutchman, and Isolde, Parsifal, and the Ring of the Nibelung tetralogy, which contains The Valkyrie, are among his best-known works. His work transcends his character, which was distinguished by megalomaniacal inclinations and anti-Semitic sentiments, making him one of the most divisive individuals in classical music.

Debussy

The father of modern classical music is frequently referred to as the French composer Claude Debussy. Debussy created new, intricate musical structures and harmonies that are compared to the works of his contemporaries, the Symbolist and Impressionist painters and writers. La Mer, then Prelude to the Afternoon of a Faun, Clair de lune, and the Pelléas et Mélisande are just a few of his notable compositions.

Tchaikovsky

Pyotr Ilyich Tchaikovsky turned out to be one of the most well-known Russian composers of all time by creating music with a broad emotional appeal throughout the Romantic era. He received his education in the western European tradition and incorporated distinctive Russian musical components into French, Italian, and German styles. His most well-known pieces include Minor, Op. 23, Piano Concerto No. 1 in B-flat, and Marche Slave, Op. 31, as well as Swan Lake, The Sleeping Beauty, and The Nutcracker, all of which were written for the ballet.

Chopin

In the Romantic era, Frédéric Chopin was a French pianist and composer from Poland. He was one of the few composers to focus exclusively on one instrument, and his precise handling of the keyboard allowed him to fully use the piano's capabilities, including new finger and pedal techniques. As a result, he is most known for his piano compositions, such as Heroic Polonaise, Nocturne, Op. 9 No. 2 in E-flat Major, and Nocturne in C-sharp Minor.

Haydn

One of the key figures in the 18th century's development of the Classical style of music was the Austrian musician Joseph Haydn. He contributed to the development of the string quartet and symphony's forms and aesthetics. Haydn was an amazing composer, and some of his best-known compositions include the Cello Concerto No. 2 in D Major, the Emperor Quartet, and Symphony No. 92 in G Major. His works are frequently described as humorous, graceful, and lighthearted.

Vivaldi

Italian violinist and composer Antonio Vivaldi lived during the Baroque era. He composed music for operas, solo instruments, and small ensembles, but his concerti, in which virtuoso solo parts alternate with sections for the entire orchestra, are what is most frequently remembered. His best-known composition, a quartet of violin concertos named The Four Seasons, is one of the approximately 500 concerti he wrote. He is similarly whimsical and intricate in his Concerto for Two Trumpets in C Major, Op. 3, No. 10, Concerto for 4 Violins and Cello in B Minor, Op. 3, and Mandolin Concerto in C Major, RV 425.

Getting To Know Your Instrument

The first step on a very rewarding journey is deciding to learn the piano. The good news is that you won't travel there by yourself. You'll have access to an instrument for learning. It will be a constant source of fulfillment, a calming presence in your house, and a valued companion. So let's locate the ideal instrument for you. Even a quick search might turn up a wide variety of options and terminology, which can be a little overwhelming. We're prepared to assist. This chapter equips you with all the knowledge you require to select the ideal keyboard or piano for you. Take a look at the fast buyer's guide at the conclusion of this chapter if you don't need all the details. Let's begin by classifying your choices into three groups:

- Electronic keyboards: The least expensive, most practical, and most adaptable. Keyboards are a good introductory instrument even though their sound and feel aren't as good as that acoustic pianos.
- Electronic pianos: More pricey and bigger, yet almost as versatile and close to the sensation of an acoustic piano. If finances and available space permit, a wonderful substitute.
- Acoustic keyboards: The largest and most expensive option and the one that offers the best playing experience and sound quality.

Understanding an Electronic Keyboard

The simplest option is a keyboard, which consists of a case surrounding the keys and buttons. This makes it transportable and typically the less expensive choice. Because the sound is either created or sampled, the keyboard may also be referred to as an "electric" or "electronic" keyboard. It is produced by an internal speaker with volume control (or a headphone input if you don't want to be bothered).

The bare minimum choice is a keyboard. This makes it portable and frequently the least expensive choice. Digital keyboards are easy to maintain and offer a wide variety of instrument sounds, including pianos, organs, and non-keyboard instruments like strings. Cheaper, older keyboards have poorer sound quality than more recent models. The playing experience on digital keyboards can vary greatly depending on two important factors: the number of keys and the type of key actuation.

Number Of Keys

The 88 keys of a full-size piano keyboard cover seven octaves and three additional notes. Choose this if you want the most accurate piano experience. The next largest is acceptable if your options are limited by size (76 keys: six octaves, three notes). This will be helpful to you, but you will discover that you are reaching the lower limit on several classical songs, such as Beethoven's "Für Elise," and the upper limit on a lot of Chopin's music (he adored the high notes).

Any fewer keys, and you'll frequently reach the upper or lower limitations. Of course, if you don't have the room and have to choose between 61 keys and nothing at all, 61 keys are the obvious choice. You will be constrained by five octaves, but that was all that was available in the 1700s when Mozart began writing music. And if Mozart approved, then it must be decent.

Major Action

This phrase describes the part of a piano that generates sound. Digital keyboards and pianos use a variety of approaches to simulate the heavier touch and feel of an authentic piano's keys because they lack the same physical components as a genuine piano. Better tools accomplish this by incorporating or reproducing versions of the

Hammer action: The most expensive and best-quality option. A mechanical hammer is moved by each key, creating a sound that is quite similar to that of an acoustic piano.

Weighted Keys: Weights are incorporated into the keys to giving them a realistic piano-like feel.

Spring-loaded action combined with weights fastened to the keys is known as semi-weighted action. Certain dynamic loss is acceptable for a debut instrument.

Unweighted Action: Typically, spring-loaded plastic keys have been molded into resistance. The cheapest choice, which is accessible on many synthesizers.

Equipment for keyboards

Sustain pedal: Piano pedals are foot-operated levers with numerous sound-affecting features. They are already attached to an acoustic or digital piano, but if you choose an electronic keyboard, you will also require a sustain pedal (sometimes known as a "damper pedal"). The cost of sustain pedals varies according to how durable they are. The finest option is a substantial metal "piano-style" lever pedal that is weighted to feel as though it is actually connected to a piano. However, small, square plastic pedals are also acceptable if you're on a tight budget. Remember that these lighter pedals may slip a little bit and include an on/off switch that prevents them from being used subtly.

Use a keyboard stand instead of placing your keyboard on a table to correct your playing posture and technique. A keyboard does not come with a case to elevate it up, unlike an acoustic or digital piano. Instead of settling for placing it on a table, use a keyboard stand to make sure it is at the proper height and improve your posture. Strong, stable stands will feel better and won't distract you while you play with your feelings by rocking back and forth. See Chapter 3 - Proper Piano Technique for further information on adjusting the keyboard height.

Digital Pianos

The playing sensation of an acoustic piano is very successfully recreated by digital pianos, especially as technology advances. They offer the convenience and versatility of a keyboard. They are often made of wood or an imitation material and contain hammer action keys. They don't need to be tuned or maintained physically in the same way that an acoustic piano does, but this gives you the impression that you are using a solid instrument.

Similar to a digital keyboard, which provides a variety of piano and other instrument sounds, the sound is either manufactured or sampled. They feature all 88 keys, unlike many digital keyboards, so you won't be limited in what you can play. Although they come in a variety of sizes and shapes and are smaller than their acoustic counterparts, one drawback is that they are not very portable. As a result, if you choose one of these, you might need to experiment with where to put it in your house. Digital pianos often cost more than keyboards but far less than an identical acoustic piano.

MIDI USB connectors

A Musical Instrument Digital Interface, which enables you to connect a computer or portable device, is nearly always included on digital keyboards and digital pianos. This enables you to access more sounds, record your playing, and use other features of piano-learning software through apps and other programs.

Understanding The Acoustic Keyboards

The unique tone and playing style that has influenced Western music for ages. You can feel the sounds resonating as you play, up through your fingertips and throughout the space. Electronics, sampling, or loudspeakers are not used in the creation of this "acoustic" sound; instead, only physical components are used.

The disadvantage of acoustic pianos is that they are by far the most expensive option, and the cost is not just for purchase. A piano costs money to move, and they require upkeep. Acoustic pianos require routine tuning since the parts react to even tiny changes in humidity or temperature. This implies that you should think about where to put an acoustic piano. They can easily dry out and distort if kept in moist conditions or too close to a radiator.

You can view buying a high-quality piano as an investment because they maintain its value effectively. On the other hand, cheap, used instruments should be avoided because they are frequently damaged and expensive to fix. Before purchasing any instrument, you should always seek professional advice, but used pianos require extra consideration. There are numerous possibilities online for renting a piano or hiring a practice space with a piano if you're set on an acoustic piano but aren't sure you want to study in the long run. There are two types of acoustic pianos: one is grand pianos and upright pianos. Acoustic pianos have strings, hammers, and dampers inside. Over three centuries ago, in 1709, the type of piano action that is employed in modern pianos was created.

Analyzing An Acoustic Piano's Mechanics

The common piano sound is made by a hammer striking a string after a key is pressed. The hammer mechanism gives the key resistance against the finger (keyboards with "hammer action" mimic this tactile sensation). The air around the strings inside the instrument vibrates as a result of the strings. Reverberations result from this, and they pass through carefully planned holes in the piano's body and bounce about the casing. Technology is improving quickly, despite the fact that it is really difficult to fully replicate the experience of playing an acoustic piano using references, samples, or synths. All physical components of the sound, including the sound of the dampers muting or releasing the strings, are very well simulated by contemporary digital pianos. Even a low-end acoustic piano can sound and feel better than a good digital instrument.

A Large Piano

You may have seen this famous, long, low, curving piano in performances or in films of well-known classical pianists. The horizontally wound flat strings give the casing its distinctive form. As a result, the key pushes back on the fingers with a completely natural-feeling force because the hammer simply needs gravity to fall back from the string. The high dynamic range creates a rich tone that is audible in both quiet and loud environments, such as a living room or a huge performance hall. The recognizable grand piano can be seen all over the world. The original pianos were largely made for European Royal families and were initially seen as a sign of wealth and prestige.

You have access to this volume range when you touch the keys. You are forced to either pound the keys or hardly hear the notes due to low dynamic range. The smooth transition between loud, quiet, and any other volume is made possible by a high dynamic range. You may play with genuine passion and emotion if you have good control over your dynamic range. Beethoven's "Moonlight Sonata" comes to mind. The tune has subtle contrasts between soft and strong sounds throughout when played effectively. The top musicians can even change dynamics while playing many notes at once because they have such excellent control over their dynamic range.

How To Use A Piano?

Forget about the keyboardists you see sitting up. The ideal position for a pianist is to sit at the piano, and having a seat or stool that is positioned at the right height is crucial. Larger, heavier stools are often more expensive but remain comfortable for longer. Make sure the height can be adjusted so you can sit in a position that promotes good posture. Use a metronome (optional) to keep time with the tempo (speed) you have set. A metronome emits an audible sound, typically a click or a beep. Although you don't definitely need one, it can be beneficial in the beginning if you see that your pace is varying. It can be difficult to keep time without a count if you develop the habit of listening for one all the time. There are usually metronomes built into keyboards and digital pianos, but if you choose an acoustic piano and require one, there are several programs available online, most of them free.

Letters To Piano Keys

There is a letter name for each key on the keyboard. The musical alphabet's letters are used to name each key. The musical alphabet consists of the letters B, C, A, D, E, F, and G. The keyboard's natural keys are given to these seven letters. There are distinct letter designations for the black keys on the keyboard as well. On the keyboard, each black key has a unique letter name that is accompanied by a sharp or a flat.

White Keys' Letter Names

Finding the names of the keys on the keyboard is easier than you would think. By using the steps below, you should be able to remember them for the rest of your life. This activity will make it simple to identify the letter of each white key. You may find the letter for each key on the keyboard by using the steps that are provided below. Just to the left of each set of two black keys is the white key, "C." The white key marked "F" is located just to the left of each group of three black keys.

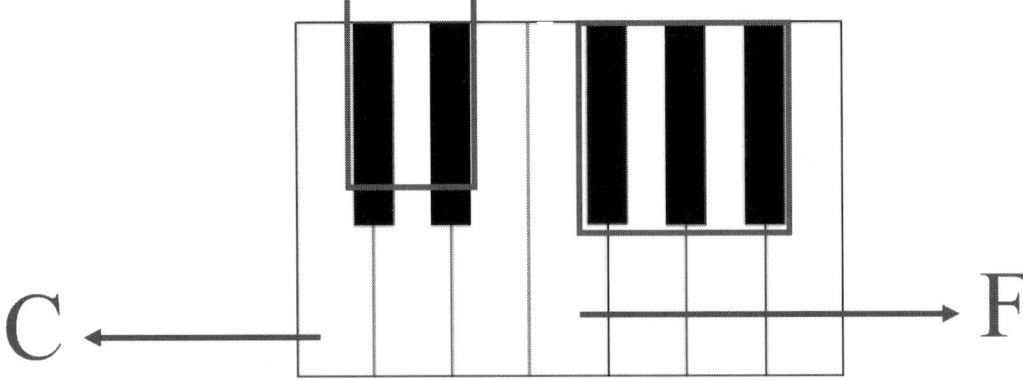

The black keys are circled in the appropriate groupings so that one may understand what is mentioned in the previous two steps. Now that you know where the "C" and "F" keys are on the keyboard, it's time to find the other letters. The letters A, B, D, E, and G must be located. Please be aware that the letter "H" is missing from the musical alphabet.

The set of two black keys contains the letter D in the center. The group of three black keys is to the right of B. Right next to the pair of black keys is the letter E. The third black key of the trio of black keys, G, is situated between the first and second black keys. Keep in mind that there is no H after G. The following white key after G is A. The second and third black keys in the set of three black keys make form the letter A. Each piano's white key is denoted by one of the following letters.

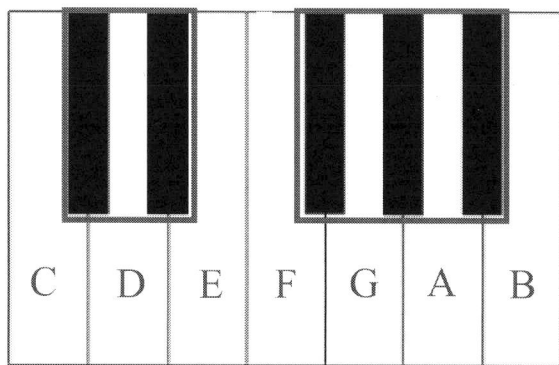

Letter Names Of The Black Keys

The black keys on the keyboard are known as sharp or flat keys. Both "#" and "b" stand for sharp and flat, respectively. Sharp on a keyboard simply refers to pressing the key immediately to the right. So, if you're on C, the black key after C is the note called C sharp (C#). D#, which comes after D, is the next key. After D sharp, the white key is E. E is followed by the white key, F. F#, the black key after F, stands for F sharp. G is the key following F#. G# comes next in the key, then A. A# is the next black key after A. Right now, we're using the keyboard. You move on to B and then C after A#. Without looking at the keyboard, you should be able to mentally match the notes to the keys. You ought to have a distinct image in your head. Develop it.

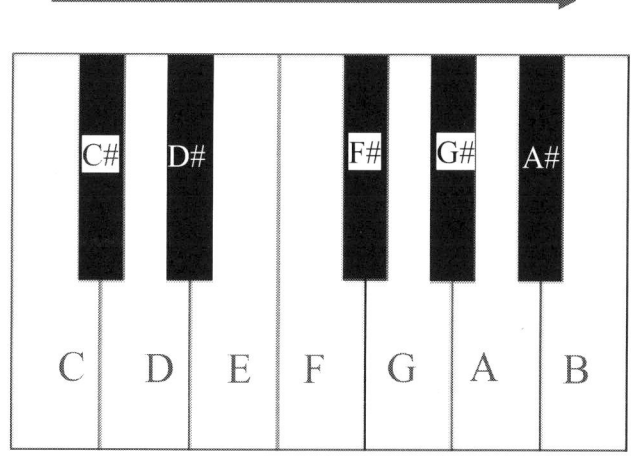

Sharps are, therefore, present when you move to the right on your keyboard (as you move up the keyboard). However, there are flats if we turn left. There are two note names on the black keys. If you're on D, D flat is the key before D. (Db). Eb is the black key before E. Going flat occurs when you are in a key and play the key to the left. You are playing G flat if you are on G and immediately play the key to the left of G. You play A flat if you are on A and are instructed to play the key that is left of A. B flat is the key before B.

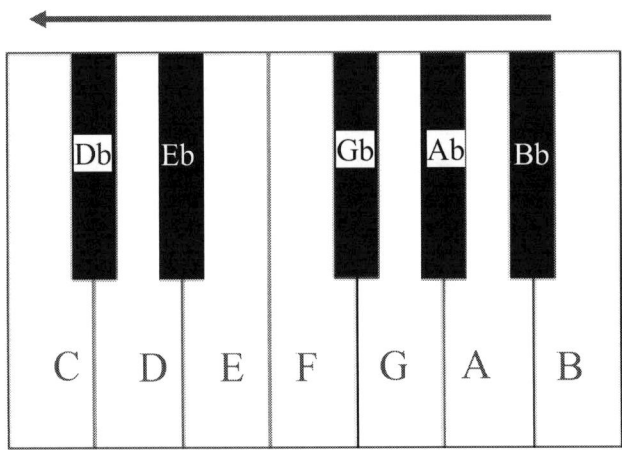

Just remember that there are 12 total keys. The first seven letters of the alphabet—A, B, C, D, E, F, and G—are used to call the piano notes. The keyboard then proceeds to display this pattern repeatedly. Middle C is frequently referred to as C4 on an ordinary 88-key piano since it is the fourth C key on the instrument. On an 88-key piano, middle C is the note that is closest to the middle.

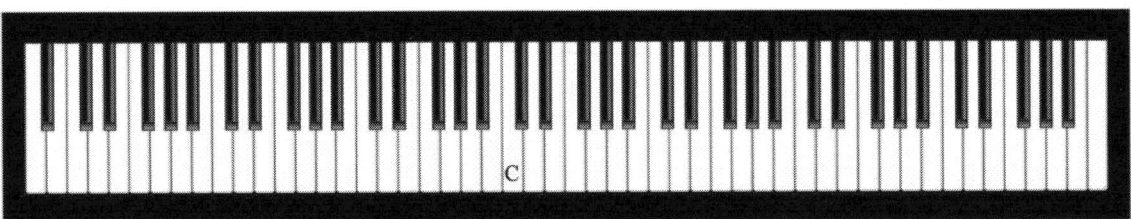

Hand Positioning

Use the tips of your fingers rather than the pads to push the keys when playing the piano. Cup your hands as if you were clutching an egg. It's simple to develop the habit of playing with flat fingers, but it will be challenging to play faster and more challenging music in the future.

When you're first starting out, holding a little stress ball can help direct your finger placement. Make it a routine to routinely check your finger placement and make any required adjustments until it feels natural. Middle C acts as your launching point as a beginner. It is the key in the center of the keyboard, the first of three white keys with two black keys between them. Your fingers should rest on the white keys on the right side of Middle C after you place your right thumb on the middle C key. Now hit the Middle C key with your thumb to play a note. In piano fingering notation, your thumb is labeled with 1, index finger with 2, middle finger with 3, ring finger with 4, and pinky finger with 5.

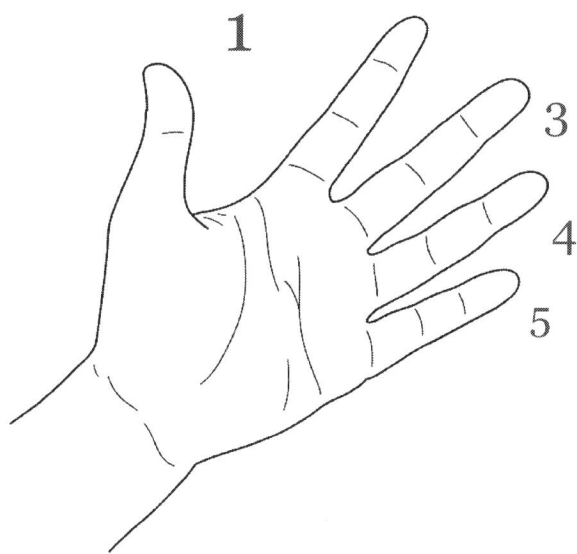

Press the white key next to it, D, with your index finger. Your middle finger plays E; your ring finger must fall on the F key. Your pinky finger play on G.

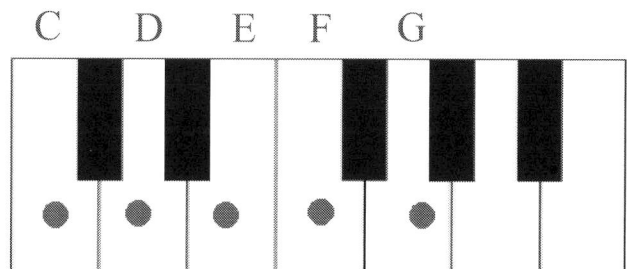

Choosing which notes to play with and which fingers will be vital once you can perform pieces. So let's immediately begin counting our fingers. B with finger 3, F with finger 1, A with finger 1, C with finger 4, G with finger 2, E with finger 5, B with finger 3, D with finger 4, and C with finger 2.

Try it now using your left hand. Practice by consistently pressing the keys, and then practice even more by following the chords listed below. As soon as you get proficient with the chords, you can combine playing several chords to produce a full symphony.

Piano Notes

A musical sound is symbolized by a piano note. On the piano, a given note corresponds to a certain key. The basis of sheet music is the notes, which determine the rhythm, pace, and pitch of the song. The pattern of a song is determined by the rhythm, which is a powerful and repetitive beat. The fundamentals of music serve as a guide for how quickly you should play each note. The tempo is the rate at which a song is played. Songs with more energy have a faster pace, whereas songs with less energy have a slower tempo. Pitch is the frequency of a note. The sound's pitch rises as a result of the waveform's acceleration with rising note frequency. To determine the duration of a certain note in sheet music, note values are used. Seven basic notes are used for each key of a piano (C-D-E- F-G-A- B). All around the keyboard, these notes are played repeatedly.

Piano Chords

A chord is just playing two or more notes at once. In other words, you create a chord by depressing numerous keys at once. The most typical keyboard or piano chord is a triad. A given chord has a root note, and two other notes are: a third and a fifth note and are also referred to as a three-note chord. You also need to comprehend spacing in order to recognize and play chords. Half-step distances are between each key. For instance, there is a half-step between the closest black key and the white key.

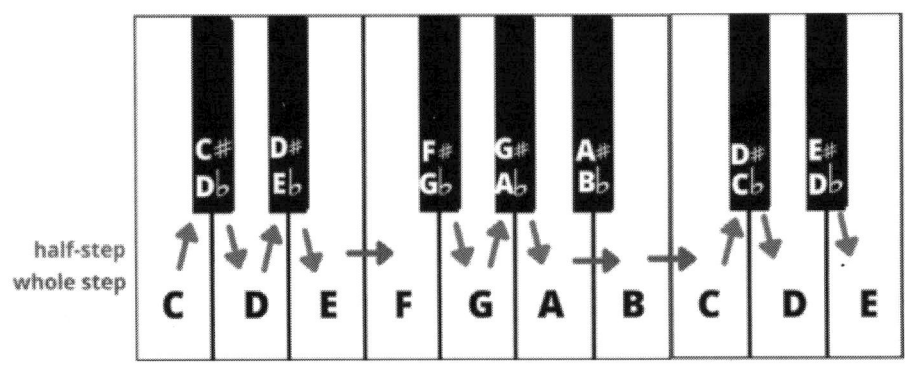

Building a shell for a chord to be played requires the root note and the fifth. Incorporate a third to complete the trifecta. Your middle finger should be positioned here.

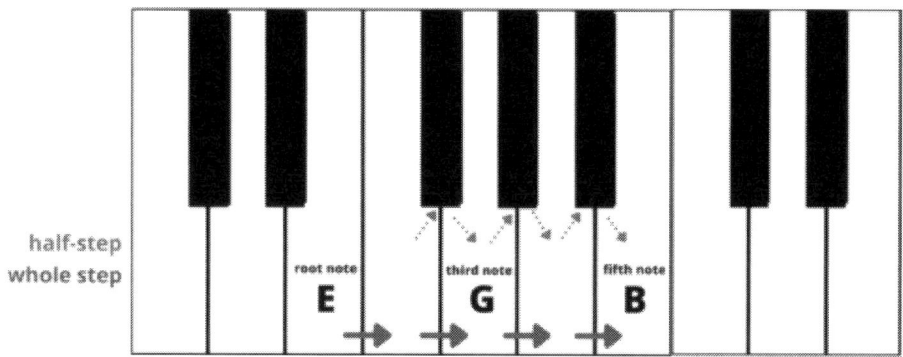

Minor Chords.

Because of their distinctive tones, minor chords arc also referred to as sorrowful chords. Because of the low tone they create, we refer to them as sad chords. Minor chords have a profound emotional impact on a song, giving it a gloomier, darker mood. Three basic notes are used in minor chords.:

- Root
- Third
- Fifth

Selecting a fundamental note should be your first step. To create a shell with the fifth, count backward eight half steps. Next, find the third note by counting three half-steps from the root.

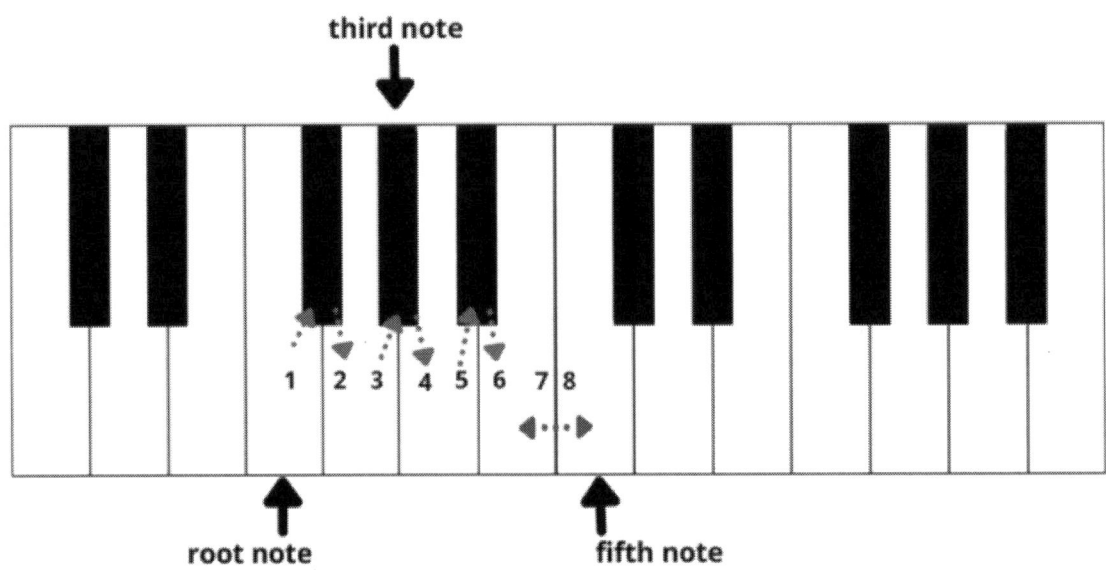

This implies that the third and not the fifth is always closer to the root note. The list of minor chords and the corresponding notes are provided below.:

"C" Minor Chord

C – Eb – G

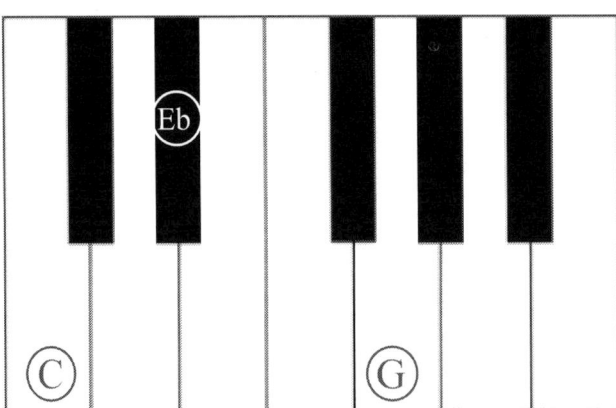

D Minor Chord

D – F -A

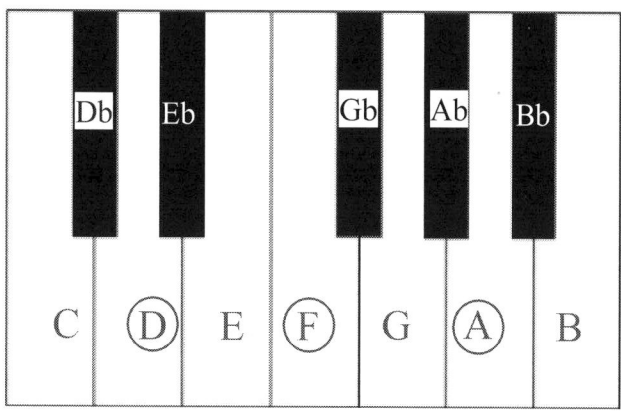

Eb Minor Chord

Eb – Gb – Bb

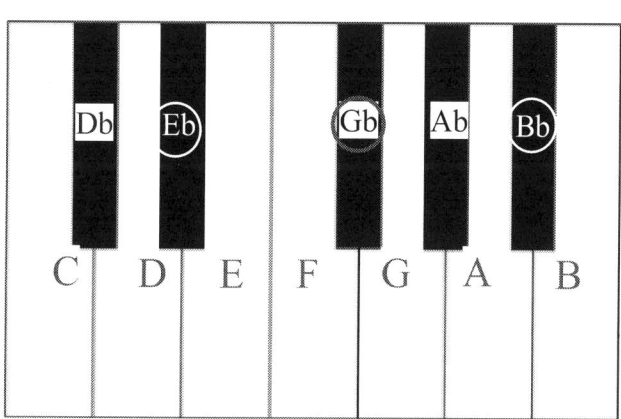

E Minor Chord

E – G – B

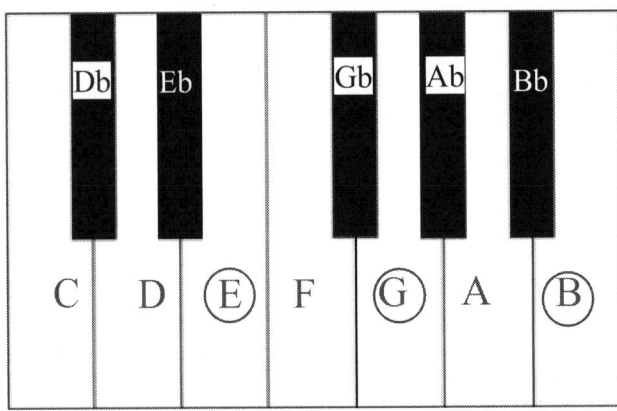

F Minor Chord

F – Ab – C

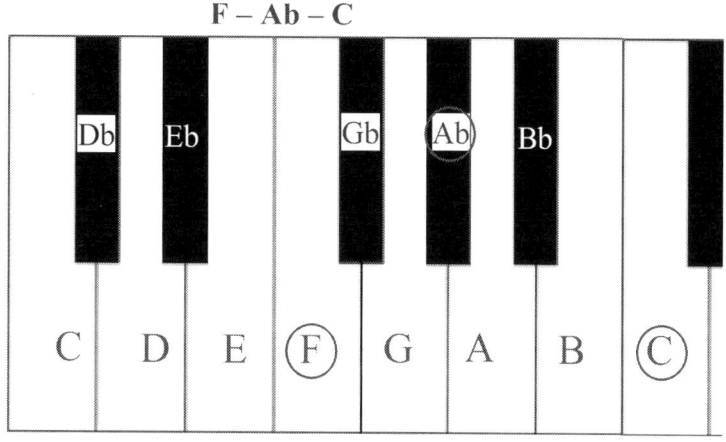

F# Minor Chord

F# – A – C#

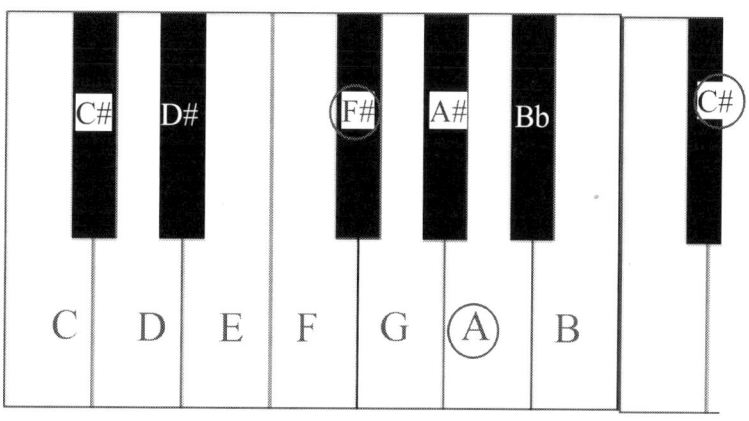

Ab Minor Chord

Ab – B – Eb

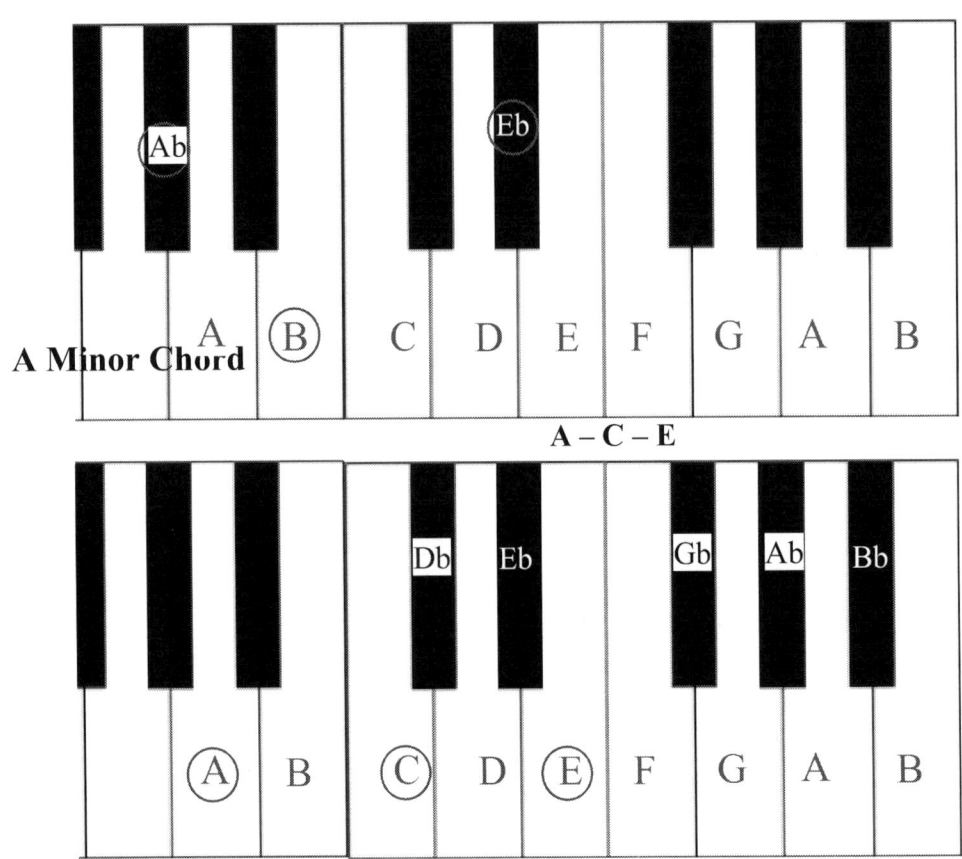

A Minor Chord

A – C – E

B Minor Chord

B – D – F#

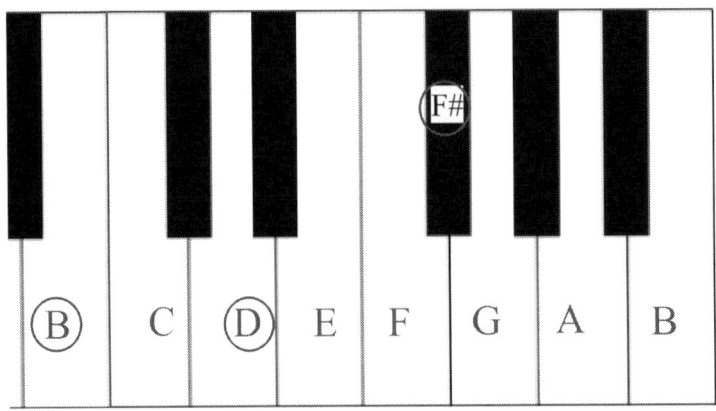

Major Chords

Because they provide bright, joyful tones, major chords are frequently heard in upbeat music. A major chord can be played in the same way as a minor chord. There is only one significant distinction. Choose a root chord first, then count seven half steps to the fifth to create a shell. However, when playing a major chord, you should place your third finger four or five half-steps from the root to the fifth.

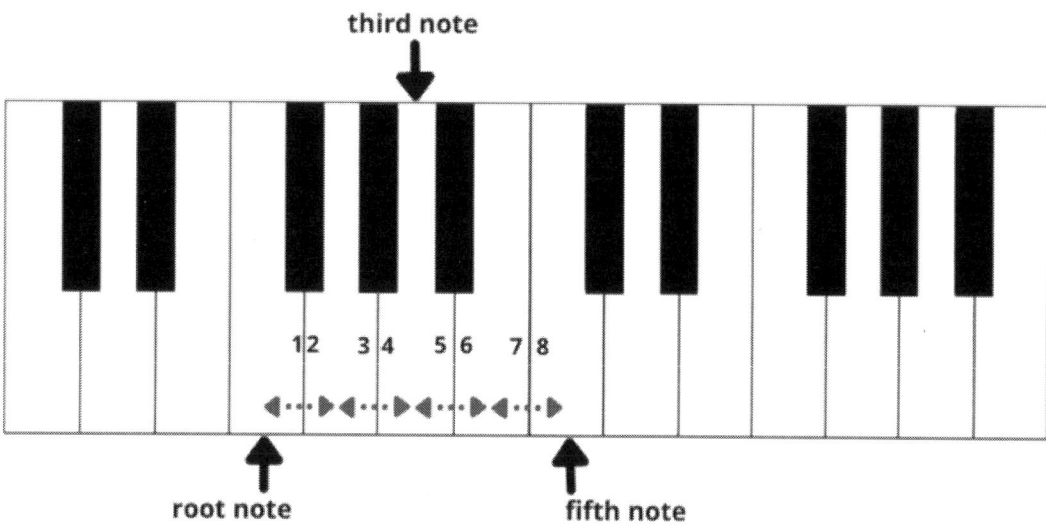

Or, to put it another way, the middle finger in a minor chord is either exactly in the middle between the root and fifth or a little closer to the fifth.

C Major Chord

C – E – G

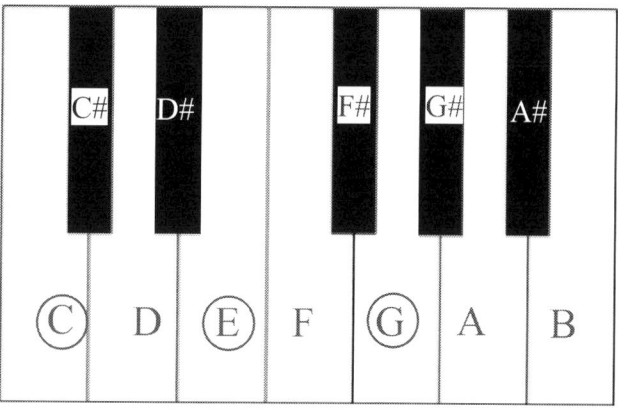

D Major Chord

D – F# – A

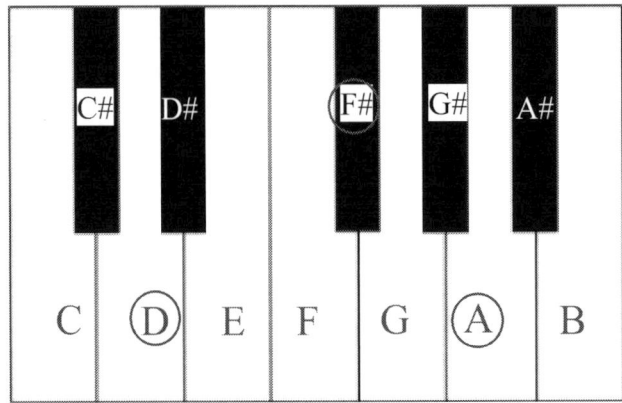

E Major Chord

E – G# – B

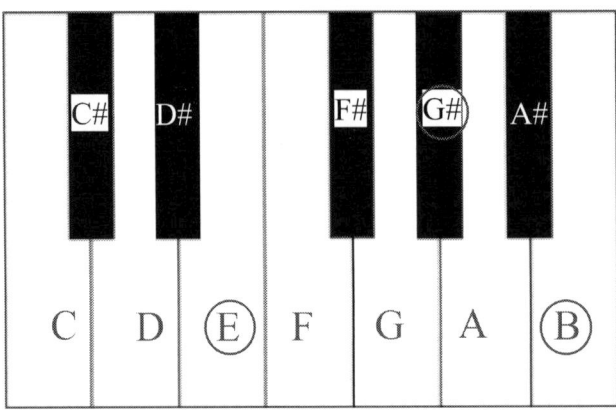

F Major Chord

F – A – C

G Major Chord

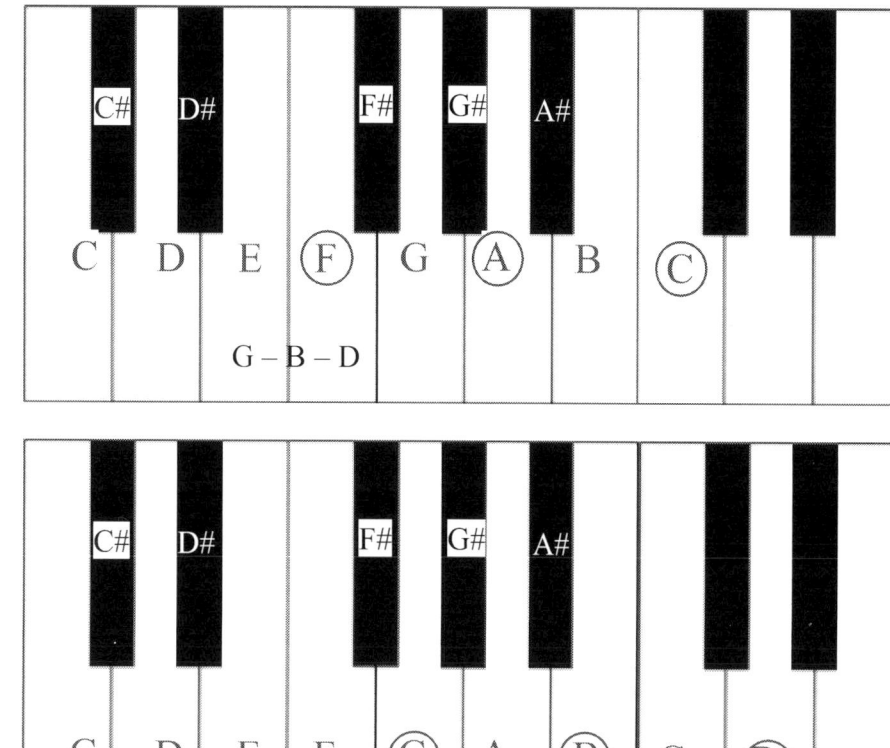

G – B – D

A Major Chord

A – C# – E

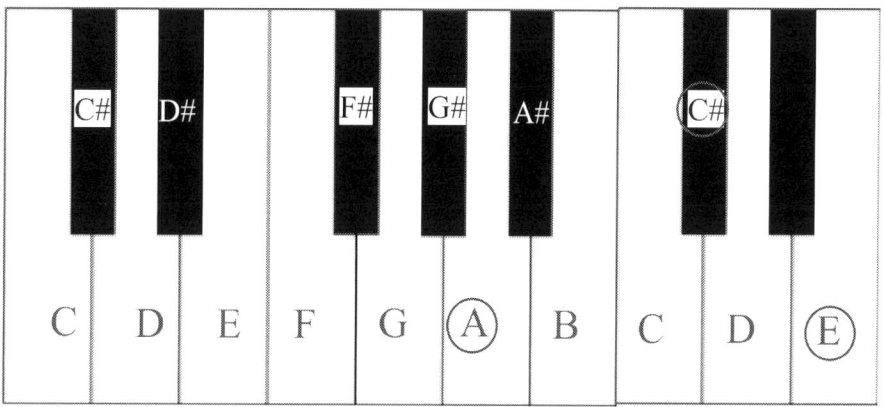

Piano Scales

Groups of notes known as scales often cover a range of notes from one note of one type to another, up or down an octave. The shortest distances between notes—steps for fundamental, diatonic (7-note) western scales—are used to separate the notes in a scale (or 2nds). We analyze two different sorts of steps: whole steps and half steps.

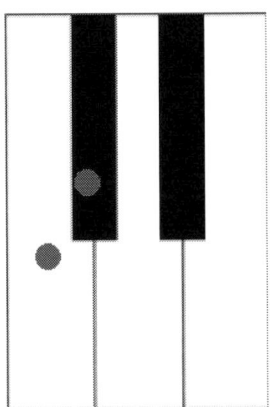   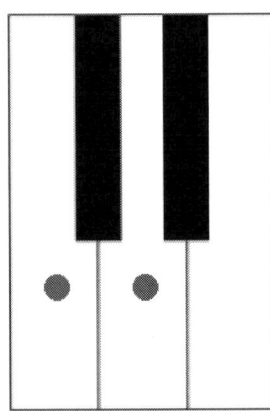

Half Step   **Whole Step**

We put a series of steps together into a regular step pattern to get the desired scale sound: For instance, the following steps are used in a major scale beginning on C: whole-whole-half-whole-whole-whole-half (abbreviated: W-W-H-W-W-W-H).

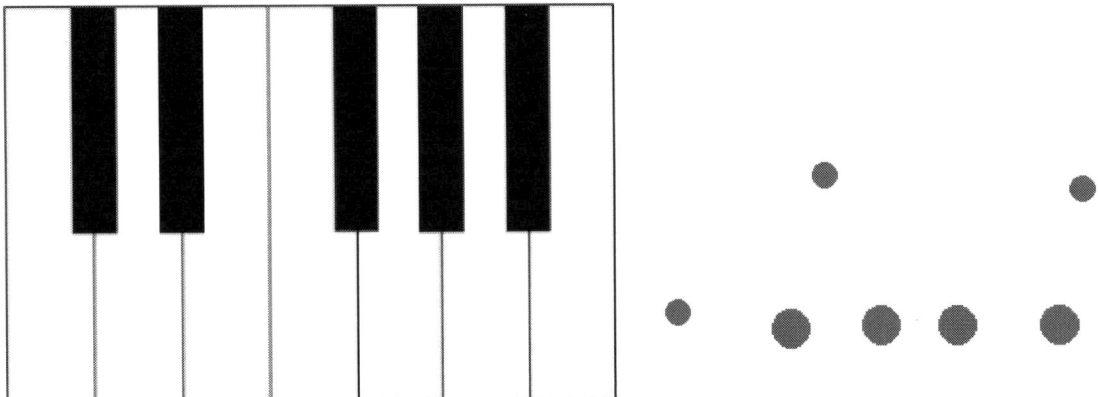

To create their sound, all major scales employ the same set of steps, even if that means switching out white notes for black notes.

Understanding The Music Sheet

Contrary to popular belief, learning to read piano sheet music is much quicker and easier than it first appears. All it takes to learn to read is to practice every day. When we do something every day, we take for granted how simple it is to learn; but when you remember yourself, every new ability is simple. Additionally, when you learn to read piano sheet music, you eliminate any uncertainty you may have regarding the song you are playing. Instead of being perplexed about what to play, the answers become clear and in front of us, allowing for more expression and experience. As long as you persevere, learning to read is fairly easy.

If you wish to participate in any kind of music theory activity, learning to read music is a necessary skill. You cannot deal with scales, chords, or rhythms in musical notation if you don't comprehend the notes on the staff. Of course, you can apply all these ideas to music that isn't written down. However, mastering the written and spoken languages can only advance your comprehension of music theory.

It may seem difficult to learn how to read music notes, but it's easier than you may imagine. All you need to do is familiarise yourself with the names of the lines and spaces on the staff, comprehend note values, and then figure out how the symbols on the page correspond to your right and left hands on the keyboard. The only thing left to do is practice, beginning with easy piano sheet music. In this section, we'll go through each of these subjects.

The sole difference between the musical alphabet and the English alphabet is that it only runs from A to G.

A B C D E F G

For pianists, the musical staff functions as a road map. There are five lines and four spaces on a musical staff. You can play on the piano by locating the notes on the lines and spaces.

Two staves are required to fit all the notes on the piano because it is so large. The treble staff is used to denote high notes, and the bass staff is for the low notes; these two staves are used in piano music (used for low notes). Each of them has a unique symbol.

Treble Staff

First, let's examine the treble staff. This staff serves as a general guide for the notes that have to be played with your right hand. You must become accustomed to the letter names for the lines and spaces if you are learning to read music notes for the first time. This is how the treble clef symbol appears:

The treble clef icon circles the G line in the figure below, as you can see. If you can recall, you can always identify the remaining lines and spaces on the staff.

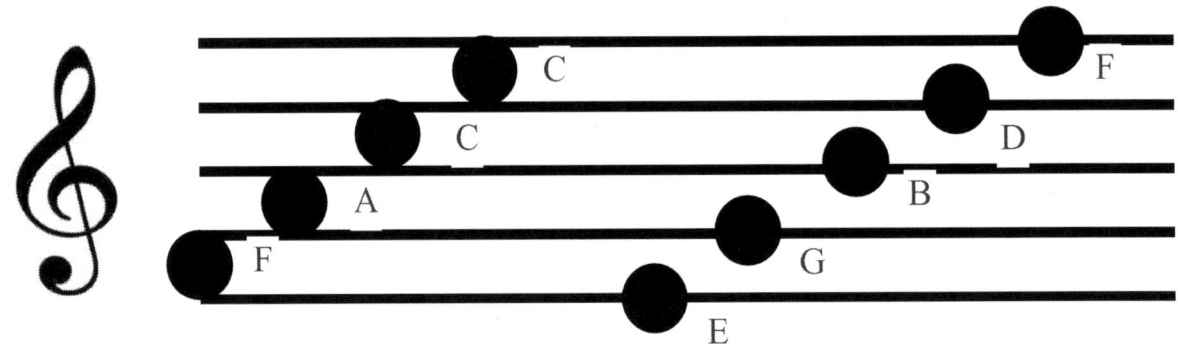

Label the white spaces on your staff paper as FACE beginning at the bottom of the page and moving up, followed by the lines EGBDF beginning at the bottom line and moving to the top line.

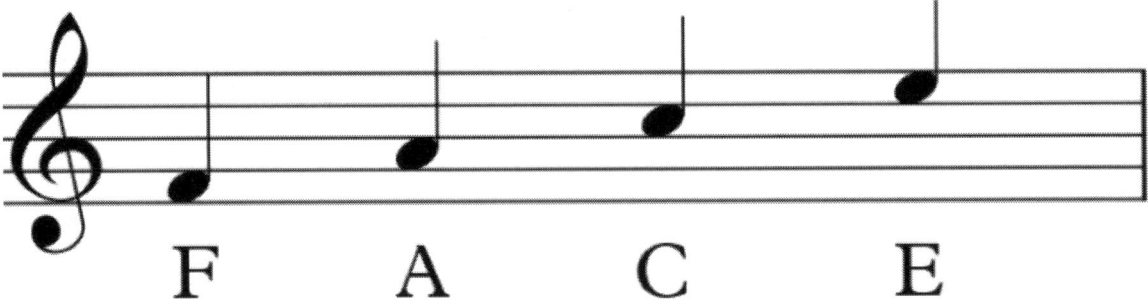

There are simple methods to aid with your memory of the names of the lines and spaces; for instance, merely keep in mind the idiom "Every Good Boy Deserves Fudge."

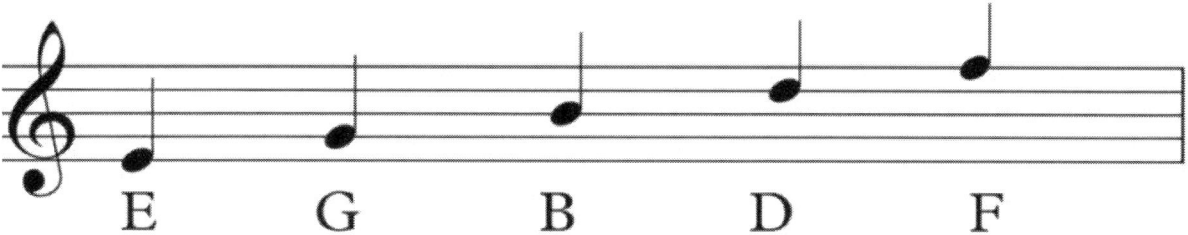

What Is The Bass Staff?

You can read piano notes on the bass staff, where the notes on the lines and spaces are often played with your left hand once you have mastered all of the letters on the lines and spaces for your treble clef. This is how the bass clef symbol appears.:

The bass staff symbol has two dots on the top and bottom sides of the F line, as you can see. If you can recall, you can always identify the remaining lines and spaces on the staff.

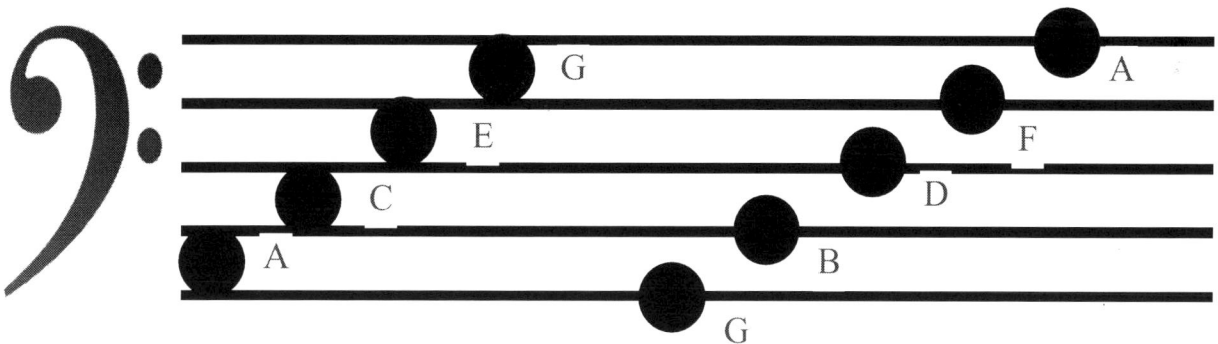

Draw the bass clef by hand. After that, label the blank areas at the bottom of the page ACEG (remember: "All Cows Eat Grass"). Next, give your lines a name, starting with GBDFA ("Good Boys Deserve Fudge Always") at the bottom of the page.

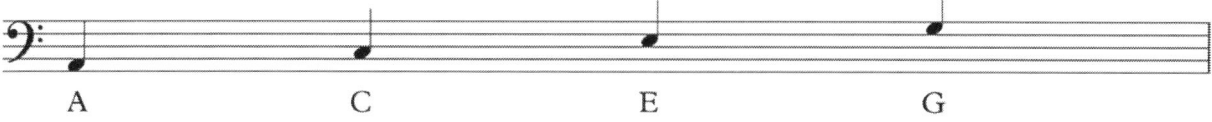

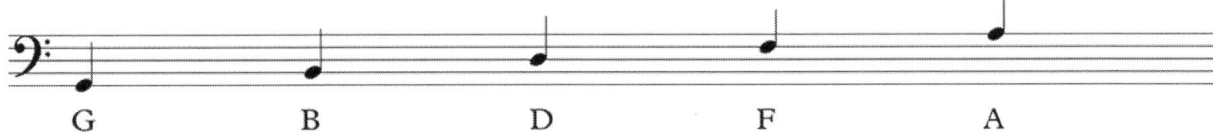

G   B   D   F   A

Let's combine the treble and bass clef staves!

The treble and bass clefs are often located on top and bottom of two staves that are piled one on top of the other in piano sheet music. Keep in mind that you should use your right hand to play all the notes on the treble staff and your left hand to play the notes on the bass staff. We refer to it as the Grand Staff when all the staves are displayed together.

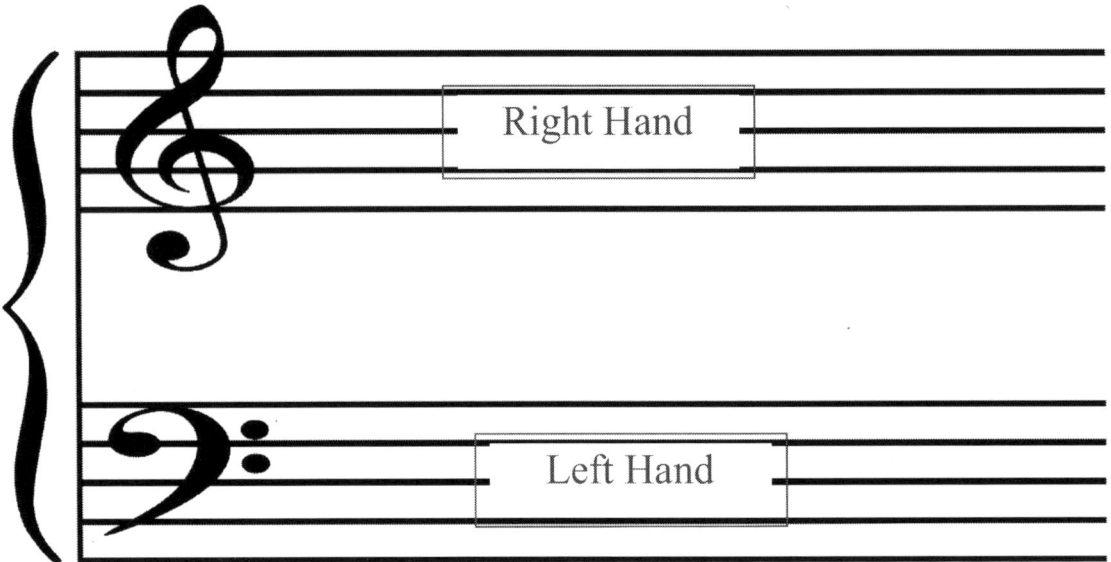

The musical alphabet simply repeats itself as it moves up the staves: A, B, C, D, E, F, G. The two staves are connected. The musical alphabet merely repeats itself by going back to A; notice that there is no H. Between the two staves, these are the only piano notes that are present.

To illustrate this, below is another picture of the piano note chart:

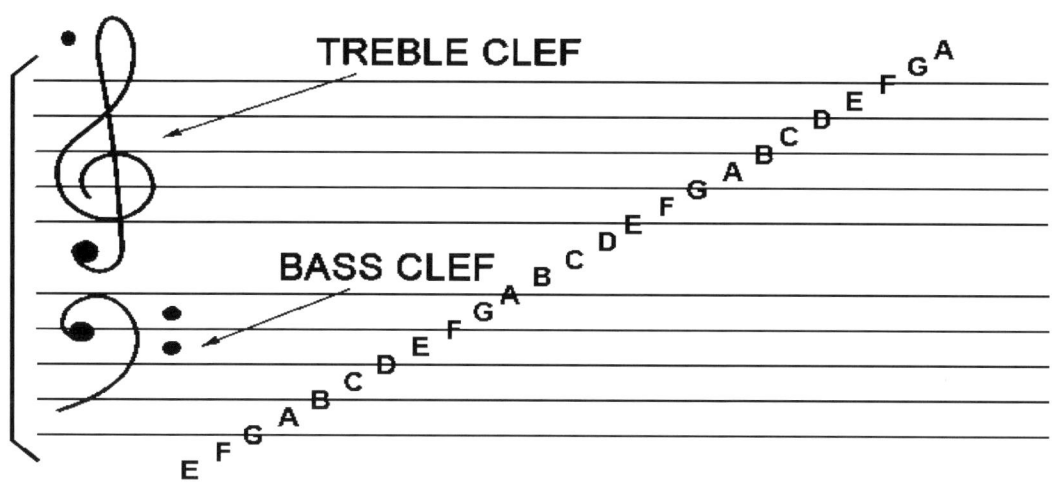

Time Signatures

A piece of music's time signature explains how it should be played. A time measure is two numbers expressed as a fraction, for example, 4/4. The bottom number describes what kind of note (such as a half note, a full note, etc.) receives one count, and the top number specifies how many counts (beats) there are in each measure. When the time signature is 4/4, for instance, the "4" on top indicates that there are about four beats in each measure and the "4" number on the bottom indicates that a "quarter note" receives one count or beat. The "3" at the top indicates that there are about three beats in each measure, and the "4" at the bottom indicates that a "quarter note" receives one count when a "time signature" is written as "3/4". We'll use the time signatures "4/4, 3/4, and 2/4" in our lessons.

Four Counts Per Measure

There are four counts in each measure of music with a 4/4 time signature. Let's begin by counting each measure from one to four. There is a + symbol between the numerals, as you can see. The word "and" can be used in place of the plus sign (+). You can count "one-and-two-and-three-and-four-and" by doing this. You will find it simpler to count an "eighth note" after learning this in subsequent courses.

Three Counts Per Measure

There are situations when three counts rather than four are used when writing music. Three counts are used in each measure of music written in the 3/4 time signature, which is also known as 3/4 time. Let's count the number of "one, two, three, and" in each measure.

Two Counts Per Measure

Other times, each measure has two counts rather than four. Two counts are used in each measure of music with a time signature of 2/4, which is referred to as 2/4 time. In each measure, let's count "one and two and.".

Note Durations And Their Representation

One of the most fundamental components of rhythm that we acquire as musicians and pianists is note duration. Duration is just a fancy word for how long anything lasts. It provides an estimated time frame for the activity. Varied notes in music are rhythmically different, which means that they vary in length depending on the type of note. What we refer to as note durations is this. When we travel, we count the miles we have to cover or use our watches to calculate the duration it will take us to drive the distance.

But in music, we count the beats or beats per measure to determine how long a note lasts. Most newcomers make the error of assuming that a beat lasts exactly one second. Never compare the tempo, speed, or slowness of musical beats to the number of seconds on a clock or watch. They are not equivalent. Beats can and frequently do last more than a second. Everything is dependent on how quickly you move. We're going to learn how to play and count quarter notes, half notes, dotted half notes, and whole notes today.

Quarter Notes ♩

With one stem linked to the side, they are filled in circles. A quarter note lasts for one beat. This implies that you will play any quarter note in your melody, or in the measure in your music, for each beat you count. If a measure has four quarter notes, you should play one of them for each beat that you play while counting a "quarter note" in 4/4 time is given one count (beat). Play each note and hold it for one count (i.e., "one and"). Count "one, two, three, and four" as well as "one, two, three, and four."

Half Notes ♩

They resemble empty circles or an open head with a side stem. A half note lasts for two beats. The half notes are twice as long as the quarter note, as you can see. You need to count and play a half note twice as long as a quarter note since a half note has two beats, whereas a quarter note only has one. When there are two half notes in a measure with four beats, the first and second beats should be applied to the first half note, and the third and fourth beats should be applied to the second half note.

A "half note" receives two counts in 4/4 time (beats). Play each note and hold it for two counts (i.e., "one and, two and"). "Count one, two, three, four, and / one, two, three, four, and"

Dotted Half Notes: ♩.

They are the next item on our list because we need to understand how adding a dot affects the length of a note. Keep in mind that every time you add a dot to a musical note, the note's duration is extended by 1/2 of what it was initially. If a half note equals 2 beats and a dot is 12 of 2, then the dot is equivalent to adding 1 beat to the half note to make a total of 3 beats. A dotted half note is played for three counts or beats when you count and play it. This is a constant fact. A dot equals one-half of the note's duration.

A "dotted half note" gets three counts in 4/4 time (beats). Each dotted half note should be played and held for three counts ("one and two and three and"), as well as each quarter note for one count (i.e., "one and"). "One-and-two-and-three-and-four-and / one-and-two-and-three-and-four and" are the numbers to be counted.

Whole Notes *O*

These large men receive four counts and beat each one. They resemble an empty circle with no stem protruding from the side, basically, a large circle. You must keep the note pressed down for all four counts in order to count a whole note. A "full note" receives 4 counts in 4/4 time (beats). Play each note and hold it for four counts (i.e., "one-and-two-and-three-and-four-and"). "One-and-two-and-three-and-four-and / one-and- two-and-three-and-four-and" are the numbers to be counted.

Eighth Note ♪

An eighth note is as long as half a beat. This indicates that there are 8 eighth notes in a whole note, 4 eighth notes in a half note, and 2 eighth notes in a quarter note (thus the name "eighth note").

Sixteenth Note

It is calculated outside of North America.

as half of an eighth note; it is also known as a semiquaver

Beamed Notes

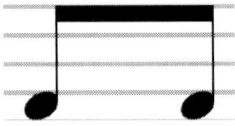

Beams can be used to connect groupings of these notes instead of flags to indicate the duration of eighth notes (quavers) and shorter notes. This can also be used to link notes in a-metrical passages. It is typically done to denote a rhythmic grouping. Eighth notes are joined together with one single beam, sixteenth notes with two beams, and so on. The number of beams is proportional to the number of flags on the note value. Beams are occasionally used in earlier vocal music printings to indicate notes that are sung on a single syllable of text (melisma). However, contemporary vocal music notation emphasizes the use of beaming in a manner analogous to instrumental engraving. Composers and arrangers can choose to use beaming to accentuate a rhythmic pattern in non-traditional meters.

Tie

Two notes of the same pitch are played as one note when they are connected together. The time values of the two linked notes are added to determine this note's length. A tie can only unite two notes of the same pitch, despite the fact that the symbols for the tie and the slur look the same.

Slur

A slurred group's first note is articulated, but the others are not. The notes on bowed instruments must be played in a single bow motion, whereas on wind instruments, the first note of the slurred group must be tongued, but the remaining notes must not—they must be played in a single, uninterrupted breath. Other instruments, such as tuned percussion instruments, connect the notes in a line as if a singer were to sing them in one single breath. Rearticulation is acceptable if a slur instead indicates that the notes should be played legato in the situation.

While the slur and the tie symbol seem the same, a slur can connect two or more pitches, whereas a tie can only connect exactly two notes of the same pitch. A slur in vocal music typically denotes that the notes beneath the slur should be sung to a single word.

An identical-looking phrase mark (or, less frequently, ligature) connects a musical section over numerous measures. A phrase mark denotes a musical phrase; however, it's not always necessary for the music to be slurred.

Glissando Or Portamento

A smooth, uninterrupted transition between notes that includes the pitches in between. Some instruments, including the trombone, timpani, non-fretted string instruments like the cello, electronic instruments, and the human voice, can create a continuous glide like this (portamento), while other instruments, like the piano, harp, or mallet instruments, blur the distinct pitches between the start and end notes to simulate a continuous slide (glissando).

Tuplet

A tuplet is a collection of notes that wouldn't often fit in the rhythmic area they are located in. The example given is a quarter-note triplet, which calls for the playing of three-quarter notes in place of the usual two. (It's often essential to look at the context to figure out how many "regular" notes the tuplet is replacing.) Although the most frequent variation is with triplets, there are other alternative tuplets that are feasible, such as five notes in the space of four, seven notes in the space of eight, etc. Duplets, triplets, quadruplets, etc., are some examples of specific tuplets that are named based on the number of grouped notes.

Chord

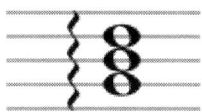

Several notes played together make up a chord. Dyads are two-note chords, whereas triads are three-note chords constructed using the third interval.

Arpeggiated Chord

A chord is made up of notes played quickly one after the other, usually ascending, and each note being held as the others are played. It can also be referred to as an arpeggio, a rolled chord, or a broken chord.

Beams And Flags

When the notes are in the same unit inside a measure and have a duration of less than a quarter note, beams are used to connect them. Beams are the preferred method for notating note values less than a quarter note in instrumental music. Although some engravers have started using beams in vocal music along with instrumental music, flags are typically employed in vocal music instead of beams.

In straight meter: Divided beats in simple meter can be linked by a beam to make the notation easier.

2/4 meter
An adjacent beat shouldn't be coupled to a beat of three notes or more.

To avoid giving the musician the impression that the whole measure is made up of a combination of dotted eighth and sixteenth notes, avoid beaming a dotted-eight and sixteenth-note with two eight notes.

3/4 METER

It is possible to beam notes from the first beat with notes from the second beat, notes from the second beat with notes from the third beat, and notes from all three beats. DON'T make a 3/4 measure appear to be a 6/8 measure by combining all three eight notes together; instead, use flags.

4/4 METER

The second and third beats must never be combined with a beam together, although beams can be used to connect divided beats with one another.

Unless there is syncopation, it must be possible to identify each half of the measure. No more than two sections of any beat should be beamed to another unit.

Never can the first two beats be combined with the last two.

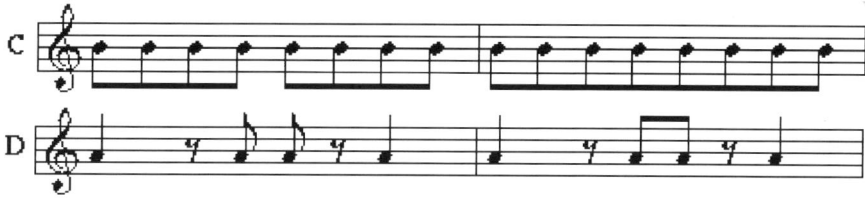

In Compound Meter

Compound meters allow for the division of each beat into thirds.

Direction Of Slant

Typically, the beam angles upward or downward to match the notes it is connecting.

The first and last notes in a group of notes decide the beam slant's direction if the notes are going in separate directions.

The beam slant is 1/2 the space in the inside notes when the initial and end notes are different, and all of the inside notes are going upward.

Amount Of Slant And Beam Placement

Never slant more than one space up or down, as a general rule. The tilt and placement of a beam are determined by three factors: within the staff and the position of a beam's horizontal spacing. The time between each beam note

Beams' Position in Relation to the Staff

Frequently, a white area in the shape of a wedge is created when beams fall within the staff. Earlier engravings had issues with this since the ink frequently leaked into the area and formed a thick wedge of ink. Engravers employed one of two techniques to get around this issue:

Place the beam either at the top of the staff line or at the bottom, or Straddle the staff line with the beam.

Stems on both notes have been shortened by 1/4 space.

Sit   Straddle   Hang   Straddle

It could be necessary to shorten stems to fill this job on the staff. Engravers may increase the slant to form a bigger wedge in order to prevent running ink if the distance between beamed notes makes it impossible to avoid one.

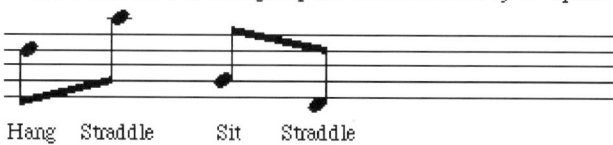

The second note in each group has been shotened by 1/4 space.

Hang   Straddle   Sit   Straddle

Any time a beam crosses a staff line, the stem or stems must be given an additional 1/4 space. Notes are spaced horizontally. The degree of the beam slant increases with the distance between the notes; the distance between the notes decreases the degree of the beam slant.

For a typical beam slant, beam notes should be spaced three to four spaces apart.

3 spaces   3.5 spaces   4 spaces

Exceptional beam slants must be used if notes are separated by less than three spaces.

Beamed notes never have a slant of more than half a space below the first leger line below the staff. (9 EVPUs), and beamed notes never have a slant of more than half-space higher than the first line above the staff. (9 EVPUs)

Intervals and their corresponding beam slant

Interval Between Beamed Notes	Slant in Spaces	Slant inEVPU's
2nd	1/4	4.5
3rd	1/2 to 1	9 to 18
4th	1/2 to 1 1/4	9 to 22.5
Octave	Up to 2	Up to 36

The thickness of the beams should be equal to half the distance between staff lines, depending on the size of the staff. When to use horizontal beams in general: when a series of notes starts and ends on the same note.

Groups of three notes:
When the central note is at its highest, upward stems.

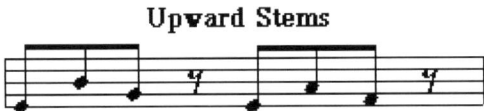

When the center note is the lowest, downward stems.

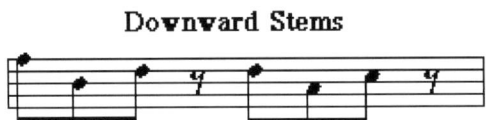

Groups of four notes:

The same interval when the notes do.

Downward stems: When the two outer notes are present on different staff degrees, and the two inner notes are a little lower than the two outer notes.

When the two outer notes are on different staff degrees and one of the inner notes is a little higher than the outer notes, and the other is lower than the outer notes.

When the first or last note is balanced by the middle note, which is lower.

When the first three notes are higher, and the final three are on the same scale degree, or when the last three notes are higher, and the first three are on the same scale degree.

Vertical Stems

When the last note is lower, and the last three notes are on the same scale degree, or the last three notes are on the same scale degree, but the first note is lower. When the two outside notes are on separate staff degrees, the two inner notes are a little higher than the two outer notes.

When there are several staff degrees for each note and one inner note is higher than the other.

The same guidelines that apply to groups of four notes also apply to groups of more than four notes.

Beams, primary and secondary

The beam that connects every note in a set of notes and is located the furthest away from the note head is known as the primary beam. A secondary beam is any beam that is located between the primary beam and the note heads. Primary and secondary beam separation: 1/4 space.

In a group of notes, stems often extend to both beams; however, some stems will only connect the primary beams to the group's two outside notes, while the stems of the inner notes only reach the secondary beam. The primary beam is symbolized as a "P" beam and a secondary beam as an "S" beam in the sections that follow.

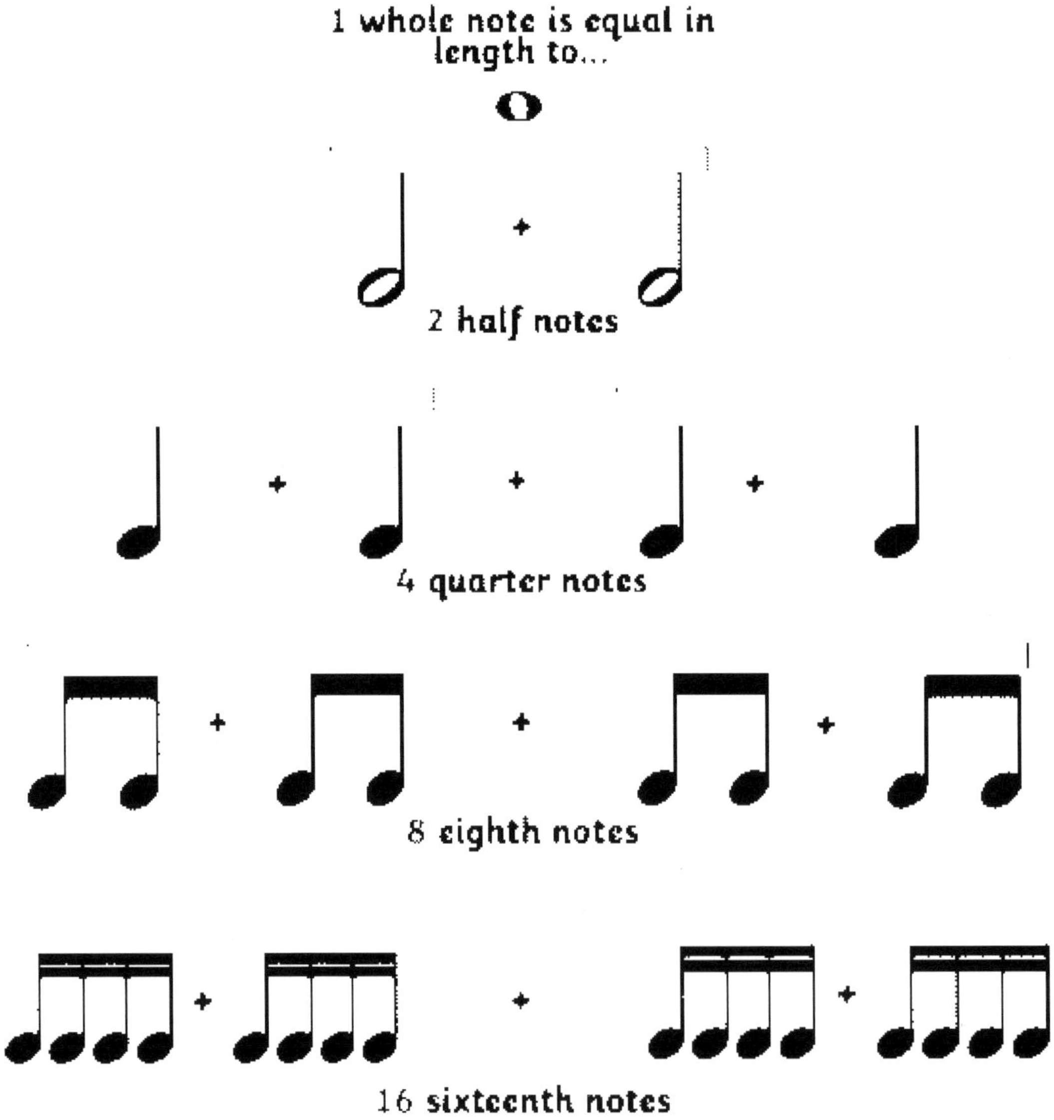

1 whole note is equal in length to...

2 half notes

4 quarter notes

8 eighth notes

16 sixteenth notes

Learning To Play A Basic Melody

Have you ever wished you could perform the piano version of "Twinkle, Twinkle, Little Star"? No sheet music is needed to learn this song because it is so simple. You can learn the easy pattern to play to hear "Twinkle Twinkle, Little Star" once you've identified the fundamental notes on your piano. You can play everyone's favorite childhood song effortlessly with a little practice. On your keyboard, locate Middle C. The middle C key on your keyboard is the "C," which is always the white key directly to the left of the two black keys. Activate the C key with your thumb.

Locate the G key. To the right of Middle C, there are four white keys. It's "G" now. the G key with your ring finger. Locate the A key. Find the white key to the right of the letter G. Its key code is "A." Place your ring finger above the A key. The keys should be hit in the following order: "CC GG AA G." Play the piano keys to "Twinkle Twinkle Little Star" in time. If it helps, try singing while you press the keys to get a better sense of the rhythm.

Take note of the three keys you have not yet identified between Middle C and A. The "D," "E," and "F" keys are those. Put your thumb over the C, ring finger above the F, middle finger above the E, and the first finger above the D. Play "FF EE DD C" as the pattern. The pitches for these keys correspond to the lyrics "How I wonder what you are."

Put on the following scene. Put your index finger on the D key, little finger above the G, ring finger above the F, middle finger above the E, and middle finger above the middle finger. Play the Up Above the World So High pitches. The following are the keys: G G F F E D For "Like a diamond in the sky," use the following pitches again: GG FF EE D. Replicate the pattern (and finger placement) you used to start the song. CC GG AA G, "Twinkle twinkle, tiny star."

Finish the song. I'm curious about who you are, FF EE DD C.

Put the music as a complete together. Write the musical letter names of the notes on some paper and place them above or below the keyboard keys if you are having problems recalling them at first. As you play, keep an eye on the page until you have mastered the song.

Music Sheet

Use the following music sheet to read the notes, and arrange the fingers in accordance with the finger numbers provided for each note. By this point, you should have read all the directions, piano music sheet jargon, and terminology related to it. Practice now!

Twinkle Twinkle Little Star

Beginner Version

Arranged by Ben Dunnett

Learning Mary Had A Little Lamb On The Piano?

"Mary Had a Little Lamb" is among the easiest songs to play, whether you're a beginner or introducing a young child to the piano. Only three notes make up the basic melody, which is played with just three fingers on the right hand. The simplest key to play in is C major, so start there. From there, you can progress to harmonizing chords and more difficult variations that are played with both hands or in various keys.

Playing in C Major

- Put your right hand in the C position, starting with the thumb. Use the white middle C key (in the center of the keyboard) and the two keys to its right to play "Mary Had a Little Lamb" in C-Major. D and E are these.
- You can play the first five notes of the C major scale in the C position: C-D-E-F-G. Your pinky will play G while your thumb is on middle C.
- These are the sole notes you'll use for the fundamental melody in C major. With just these 3 keys, you can play the entire song, though you can be more creative with it once you get the fundamental melody down.
- Perform E D C D E E. The song's opening line is composed of these notes. Sing along to the song's lyrics, "Mary had a tiny lamb," as you play. Every syllable has its own sound. The third line of the song begins with these notes; thus, once you understand that phrase, you have already heard the first half of the first verse.
- Even though you can play this tune with just one finger, you should practice using all three fingers to get acclimated to it. You'll need this ability if you later want to try playing more difficult arrangements or adding chords.
- Play D-D-D-E-E-E to move to the second line. Little Lamb, Little Lamb is the song's second line, and it is simply the final two notes you played for the first line of the music, each repeated three times. You can also play D-D-D-E-G-G as an alternative, pressing the G key with your pinky.
- Now add the third line, which is the same as the first line, once you've played the second line.
- For the final line of the verse, play E-D-D-E-D-C. As with the other lines of the song, you play one note for each syllable of each word in the final line's lyrics, "its fleece was white as snow."
- Play "Mary Had a Little Lamb" after finishing the final line by trying to continuously play the next four lines: E-D-C-D-E-E-E / D-D-D-E-E-E / E-D-C-D-E-E-E / E-D-D-E-D -C.

For the subsequent verses, use the same melody. Of course, the song "Mary Had a Little Lamb" has multiple verses. The notes used in each stanza, however, are the exact same throughout. You can play the entire song once you have mastered the first verse.

Method 2: Harmonizing the Melody

Find chords that go with each note. Each note in the piano's major scale corresponds to a harmonizing chord. The root note is where the chord is. Then, playing in every other key, add two notes above that one.

For instance, the C major chord, which is made up of the notes C- E, and G, is the harmonizing chord for the note C.

If you're teaching a young child to play the piano, this is an excellent chance to incorporate some music theory into your session in a useful, hands-on approach that they will probably pick up very quickly.

Form a chord with your hands. Simply move the hand up and down the piano while playing three notes at once to play chords as opposed to just one note. While playing, maintain the same position for your hands.

So that you don't have to use any black keys, start with C major. Before you can harmonize the melody in other scales that call for the use of black keys as well, you might need to practice.

Your fingers should be slightly bent into the same form as your wrists. You shouldn't have overly clawed or rigid fingers.

Play the melody while moving your entire hand. Simply play the harmonized chord rather than the single note to play a harmonized melody. When playing in this manner, your thumb will always be on the chord's root note, which corresponds to the melody's initial single note.

Try playing the entire tune with just your thumb while you're first starting out (but without engaging the other fingers). As you play the tune, you will become accustomed to moving your hand up and down the keyboard.

Method 3: Trying Variations of the Same Tune

To play the song in G major, move your hand. Simply move your hand up the keyboard until your thumb falls on the G key if you wish to play "Mary Had a Little Lamb," where your pinky finger is in the C position. While playing in G major technically requires the use of black keys, the basic melody can be played without them. Use the same technique you did when you played the song in C major as long as you're playing the core melody.

When performing the song in D major, use F sharp. To play D major, position your hand such that your thumb is on the D. Use F sharp instead of F, the black key to the right of F when playing the first five notes of the D-major scale. Repeat those five notes several times to become used to using the black key.

Since the melody's opening note is an F sharp, the pattern begins with your middle finger. You simply continue using your fingers in the same manner from there.

You may learn to transpose songs into other keys by writing down the names of the notes as you change keys. Play the tune in A major if you can. Move your thumb to the A key as you would with the other keys. The remaining first five notes of the A major scale are played with your four fingers. C-sharp, the black key to the right of Middle-C, is one of the notes.

The tune begins on the black key, the same as with D major, since the pattern begins with your middle finger. Otherwise, you perform the song in the same way you did when you played it in C major.

Use chords on the left hand to accentuate the melody. By playing the harmonizing chord while the melody is being played with your right hand, you may give the song more depth by using your left hand to play harmony chords.

In C major, go back and forth between the C major and G major chords. Move your hand 4 keys down from the C major chord to play the G major chord. As you play the song, you simply move your hand back and forth.

The chord would be put above the letter on the music notation. Traditionally, the initial note of each bar would be played on the harmonizing chord for a hymn like "Mary Had a Little Lamb." When playing softer sections of the song where you want to play more discreetly, delete the chord and add it where you want to emphasize the notes.

Music Sheet

Use the following music sheet to read the notes now that you have read all the directions, piano music sheet jargon, and term-related material. Play the notes on the Treble Staff with your right hand and the notes on the Base Staff with your left hand. Practice now!

Mary Had A Little Lamb

♩ = 80

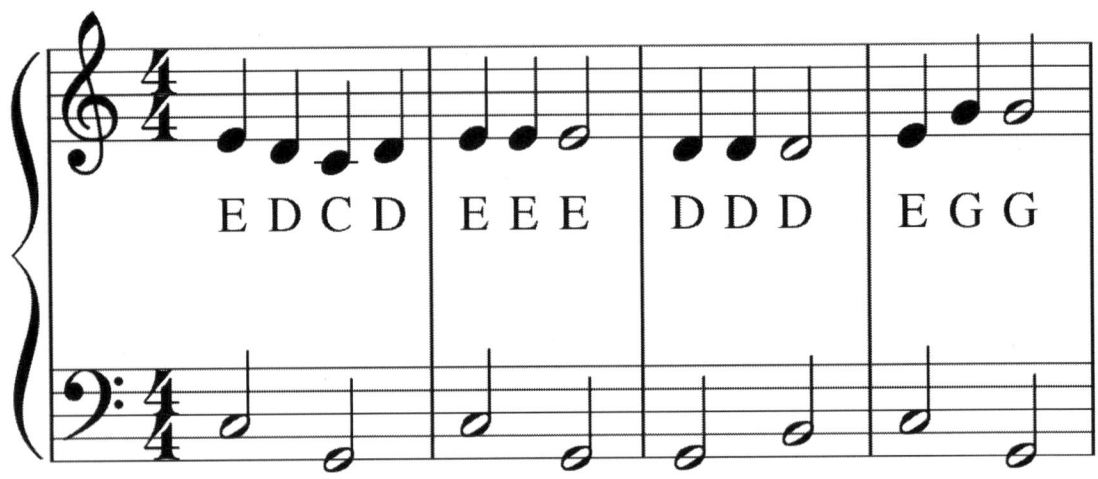

Teach Yourself Piano In 10 Steps

Remember that mastery of any instrument needs commitment to regular practise. So if you're ready to learn and determined to put in a lot of practise, let's get started. The obvious first step is to purchase a piano for yourself. Set a spending limit, research the many types of pianos, and look for deals both locally and online. Here are some things to consider.:

In music stores, renting keyboards is quite frequent. If you want to rent before you are certain the piano or keyboard is perfect for you, this could be a good place to start. Speak with any family members or acquaintances who work in the music business. They might be able to recommend someone who is scrambling to get rid of a used instrument for less money than it would cost to buy it new.

A keyboard is an excellent replacement for a piano if one is not available. They are affordable, never fall out of tune, and have a range of sounds and features that can improve your music. Not to mention, they are much easier to move around and take up very little space. A basic learning keyboard is a great tool for someone just starting out. Using these specialist instruments may help you learn songs more quickly because they light up in a specific order. They typically come with how-to guides and training films that teach you how to read music. There is always the option to start on a keyboard before switching to a piano.

Keyboards are typically less expensive than pianos. Keyboards do not get out of tune and take up considerably less space than a piano, which are both advantages. Acoustic pianos typically cost between $2,000 and $10,000, or even more, for some high-end concert grand pianos.

Become acquainted with your Musical Instrument

When you have a piano or keyboard, spend some time getting used to it. For us, play your new piano. Is it musical? Consider hiring a professional to tune it for you the first time. If you were using a keyboard, you might skip this step. Find out the names of the keys. Be sure you understand the proper hand position. Take careful notice of what each one has to say and how they differ from the others. You should practice until you can tell them apart. You want to establish good behaviors right now!

Practice Proper Arm and Hand Placement

The first step to learning to play the piano on your own is to make sure your arms and hands remain in the right-hand position. They naturally assume a cupped shape when left hanging by your side, which is known as the "C Position." You will also be able to play several fundamental piano chords with the left hand and read certain notes from the bass and treble clefs. Play five-finger patterns all over the keyboard on different keys. Make extensive use of the black keys!

Practice using the keyboard without notes to become familiar with its layout before using them to navigate.

The risk of repetitive stress injuries is decreased by having the proper hand and finger alignment. Furthermore, even though we understand that you want to learn the piano quickly, be mindful of your limitations and refrain from over-practicing.

Know Your Notes

A new musical language must be learned in order to learn to play the piano. You'll memorize this information as opposed to learning it the way you learned the letters first. With regular practise, you'll be able to memorize these in no time. The Do-Re-Mi song is a great place to start (yes, the one from The Sound of Music). Each of them, starting with pitch C, corresponds to a piano note. Thanks to it, you'll be able to master the piano's keys and note pitches.

Do – Note C
Re – Note D
Mi – Note E
Fa – Note F
So – Note G
La – Note A
Ti – Note B

To locate C, look for a set of black keys (accidentals). Directly to their left is C. The piano's Cs are separated by eight notes or an octave. The placement of F is another crucial thing to learn at first. The leftmost of the three black keys is the key. You should quickly recall your Cs and Fs because doing so makes it easier to recall where the other notes are.

Know the Difference Between Sharps and Flats

You can use the black keys to play flats (#) or sharps (b). They are arranged in pairs or trios.
When a piece has a # on it, the next higher key must be used. Ab, on the other hand, means you need to play in the key below that. Concentrate first on the middle of the piano. Do you observe the pair of black individuals as well as the trio of three black individuals? There is the C note in the center.

Two blacks are to the left of two Cs, as was previously mentioned. F, the leftmost of three blacks. You can find two notes in the middle of your piano: middle C and middle F. When pressed, the black key immediately above and next to the Middle C note either creates a C-Sharp (C#) or a D-flat (Db). The black key adjacent to it is used to play the D# or Eb. The middle F# or Gb is played on the black key adjacent to it. Do you see the pattern now? Always remember that black keys are either flats or sharps, but white keys can also play sharps or flats.

Attempt to Practice

Always consider the end when beginning. If you decide to learn the piano, what do you hope to play? When do you have this in mind? What topic will you put the most emphasis on? Is it data you found on the internet or in a book you bought? What keys or scales would you like to be able to play? What was your favorite song that you saw yourself playing when you first thought about learning to play the piano? Will you be able to play the piano in a week? 14. How 'bout thirty? Since you are merely learning how to teach yourself the piano at this point, goals longer than a month are typically unnecessary. Focus on the initial 30 days!

Start your Daily Practice

If you really want to learn to teach yourself the piano, then it is the most important step. The first three sections built up to this. Then make everyday progress! Keep up the good work. If you wish to branch out from the same few scales or chords, try these finger speed exercises. Work on your chords and scales. They will form the basis of your piano playing, so make sure to practice them every day. It's important to start with the major and minor chords. Know the fundamental keys. If you finally want to be able to play by ear and identify the sounds you generate, this is essential. Songs that are simple, like "Mary Had a Little Lamb," are ideal for this.

As you practice playing by ear, you'll start to see patterns. Each song is composed of different musical patterns. You should start identifying and comprehending these patterns as you move closer to your ultimate goal of playing songs on the keyboard or piano.

Exercise Your Fingers

Use your fingers to put the concepts into practise once you've mastered them. You can train your hands to detect objects without stumbling over them in this way. When learning to play the piano, fingering is crucial. You need to know where your fingers should go when you start playing.

A good point to start is with the pentascale technique. A pentascale is any scale that has five notes (Penta). Given that you are already aware of where the Middle C is, you may begin your finger practice with the C Major pentatonic scale.

Thumb first, then index, middle, ring, and pinky should be placed on the Middle C note. These five notes make up the pentascale. This is one of the easiest and simplest ways to practice your fingers because it teaches all of them. Now, start out slowly by employing the whole note strategy (count four beats before pressing the next key). From here, you can go on to half notes and, eventually, quarter notes.

Once you feel more comfortable, you can go up the practice ladder to take two notes at once. You'll need to use two fingers because you'll be tapping two keys simultaneously.

Choose the Correct Timing

Every note includes a count that tells you how long to push it for. The following are the three that are most frequently used in music notation:

- Whole notes (with four beats)
- Notes in quarters (with two beats)
- four-quarter notes (with one beat)

The white circles on a music sheet stand in for whole notes. These denote the requirement to hold the note for four full beats (as in one-and-two-and-three). Half notes are also represented by white circles with stems. Two beats are used to hold these notes (one-and-two). Quarter notes look like half notes, except for the darkened rings. They remain standing for one beat.

Interact with other players

After some practice, it's a good idea to find others to practice alongside or with. A more experienced pianist could be willing to practice with you if you ask them if they have any advice or methods they used to improve. Once you start to advance, give brief "performances" to people, even if it's only your family. They will tell you what sounds great and what could want a few little modifications.

Consider taking piano instruction from a professional as a final option. You will receive in-person instruction from a teacher who will hold you responsible for mastering the instrument and demonstrating the right pace for learning. Additionally, a piano teacher will hasten the process if you learn the fundamentals on your own so you can play some simple good songs you really want to learn. Once you start to advance, give brief "performances" to people, even if it's only your family.

After reading through and viewing videos on subjects like scales, chords, and finger posture, decide what you want to learn and how quickly. Set a goal for your piano playing! The final stage is to begin exercising, ideally daily. To speed up your learning, make playing with others your goal after a few weeks. Even if it's relatives, it will motivate you to work more and share their opinions on what you've discovered. Online courses, YouTube videos, and Google resources can also be used to learn how to play the piano.

Easy-To-Read Sheet Music Of Forty Songs

Beginner's Level

Happy Birthday

Kum-Bah-Yah

Traditional
Arr. Julie A. Lind

Jingle Bells

Home on the Range

This Little Light of Mine

Scarborough Fair

Red River Valley

Silent Night

When the Saints Go Marching In

Traditional
Arranged by Julie A. Lind

greensleeves

Brahms' Famous Lullaby

Can Can

Bridal Chorus

Minuet in G Major

J.S. Bach

Gesù Bambino

Intermediate Level

Für Elise by Beethoven

83

The Entertainer by Scott Joplin

Amazing Grace

Pachelbel's Canon

Johann Pachelbel (1653-1706)
Arranged by Ben Dunnett

House of the Rising Sun

The Harmonious Blacksmith

Georg Friedrich Händel
(1685 – 1759)

Trepak from The Nutcracker

Turkish Rondo

W. A. Mozart

Allegretto

98

Shenandoah

As played by Keith Jarrett (transcribed by Douglas Gould)

104

106

Danny Boy

Fred E. Weatherly

Old Irish air
arr. Mark D. Lew

say an A - ve there for me;_____ And I shall hear, tho' soft you tread a -

bove__ me,_____ And all my grave will warm-er, sweet-er be,_____ For you will

bend and tell me that you love__ me,_____ And I shall sleep in peace un - til you come to

109

J.S. Bach's Prelude in C Major

Take Me Out to the Ballgame

Jack Norworth

Albert Von Tilzer

Take me out to the ball game, Take me out with the crowd;

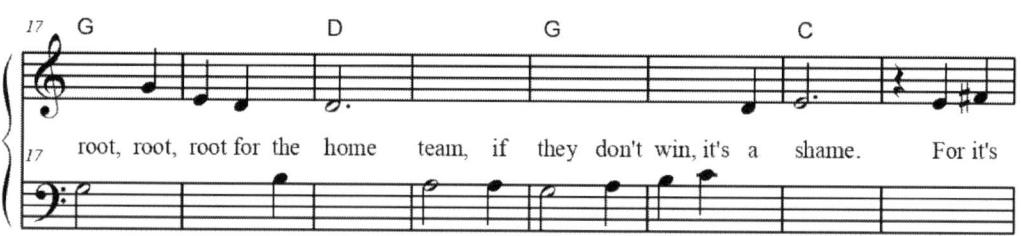

Buy me some peanuts and Crack -er Jack, I don't care if I ne-ver get back. Let me

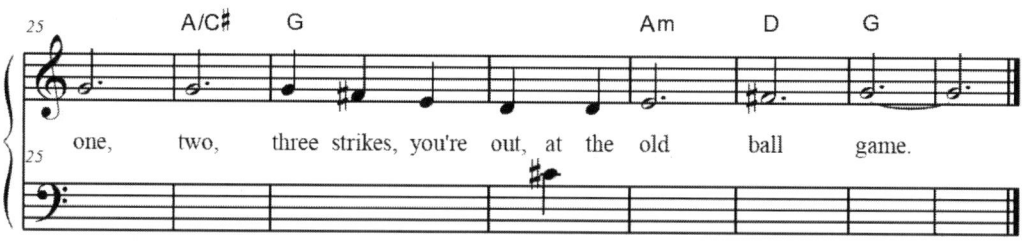

root, root, root for the home team, if they don't win, it's a shame. For it's

one, two, three strikes, you're out, at the old ball game.

New World Symphony Theme

Aura Lee

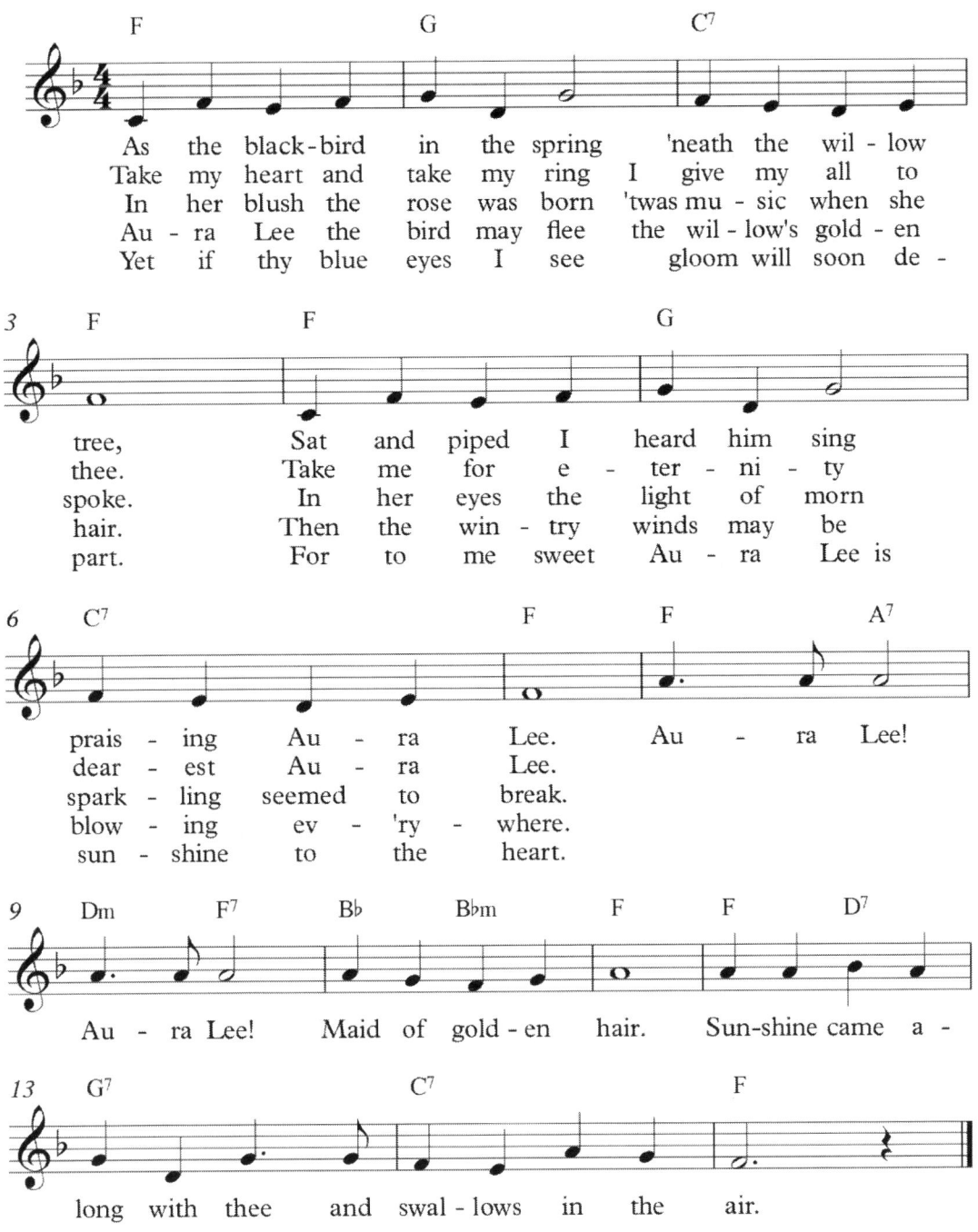

As the black-bird in the spring 'neath the wil - low
Take my heart and take my ring I give my all to
In her blush the rose was born 'twas mu - sic when she
Au - ra Lee the bird may flee the wil - low's gold - en
Yet if thy blue eyes I see gloom will soon de -

tree, Sat and piped I heard him sing
thee. Take me for e - ter - ni - ty
spoke. In her eyes the light of morn
hair. Then the win - try winds may be
part. For to me sweet Au - ra Lee is

prais - ing Au - ra Lee. Au - ra Lee!
dear - est Au - ra Lee.
spark - ling seemed to break.
blow - ing ev - 'ry - where.
sun - shine to the heart.

Au - ra Lee! Maid of gold - en hair. Sun-shine came a -

long with thee and swal - lows in the air.

Simple Gifts

William Tell Overture

Giacchino Rossini (1792-1868)

Jesus, Joy Of Man's Desiring

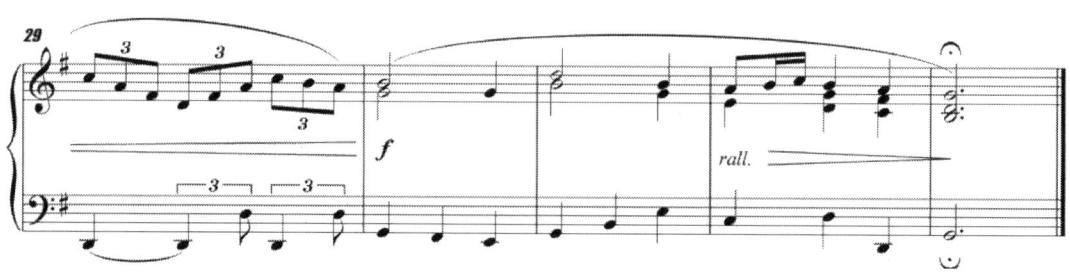

Expert Level

Theme from Beethoven's Fifth Symphony

Hallelujah Chorus

for the Lord God om - ni - po - tent reign - eth. Hal - le -

lu - jah! Hal - le - lu - jah! Hal - le - lu - jah! Hal - le - lu - jah!

For the Lord God om - nip - o - tent
Hal - le -

Hal - le - lu - jah! Hal - le - lu - jah! Hal - le - lu - jah! Hal -

reign - eth. Hal - le - lu - jah! Hal - le - lu - jah! Hal - le - lu -
lu - jah! Hal - le - lu - jah! Hal - le - lu - jah! Hal - le - lu -
Hal - le - lu - jah! Hal - le - lu -
le - lu - jah! Hal - le - lu - jah! for the Lord

Hal - le - lu - jah!

jah! Hal - le - lu - jah! Hal - le - lu - jah! Hal - le - lu - jah!
jah! Hal - le - lu - jah! Hal - le - lu - jah! Hal - le -
God om - nip - o - tent reign - eth. Hal - le - lu - jah!

Hal - le -

129

3

Morning Mood

4

Water Music

Mozart's Twelve Variations on "Ah, Vous dirai-je, Maman."

VAR. XII
Allegro

Surprise Symphony

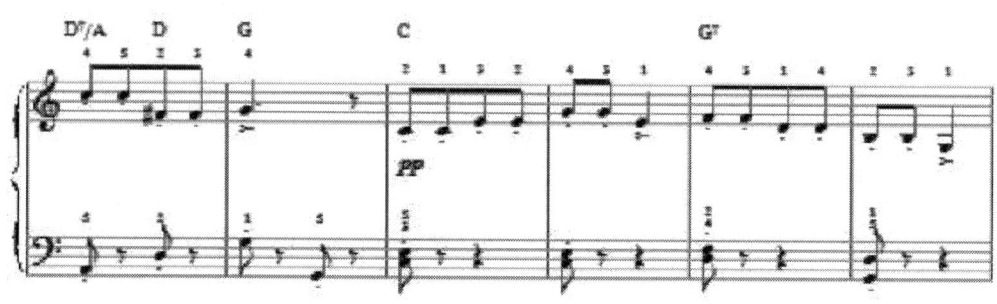

Largo from New World Symphony

Musette in D Major

150

Pavane pour une infante défunte

Très lointain

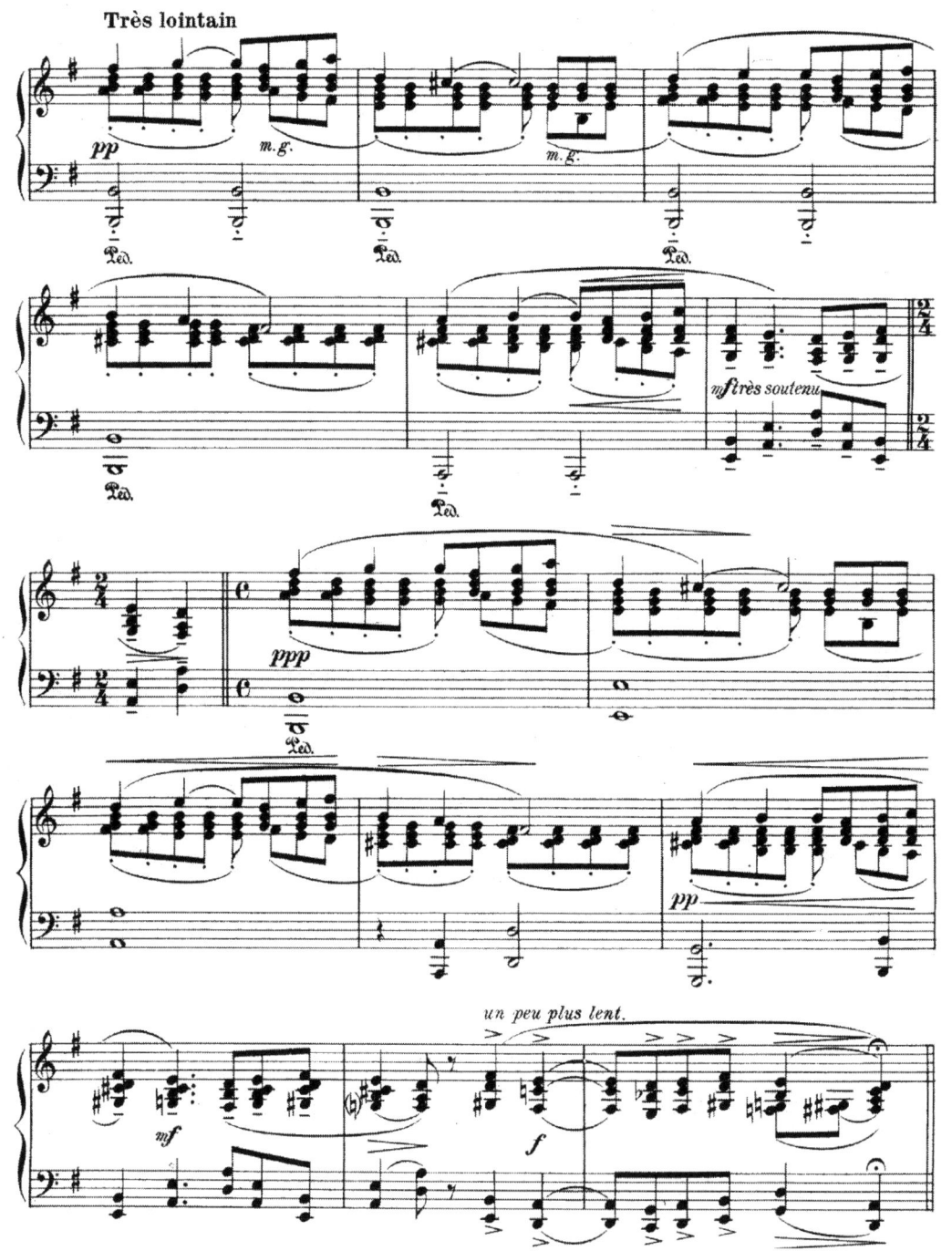

1er Mouvement

marquez le chant

Reprenez le mouvement

En élargissant beaucoup

E. 623 D.

Imp. C. G. Röder, Paris.

Liebestraum No. 3

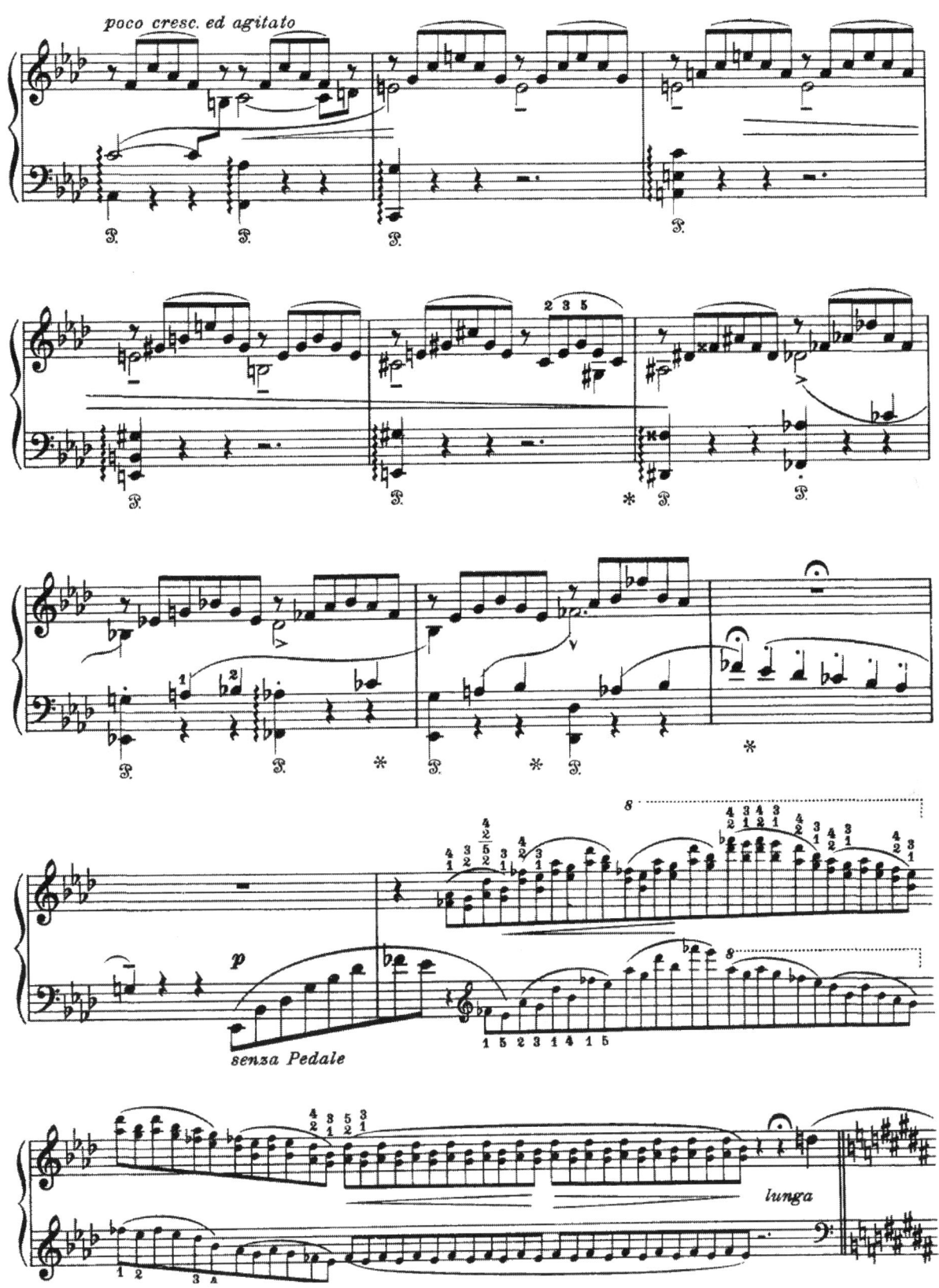

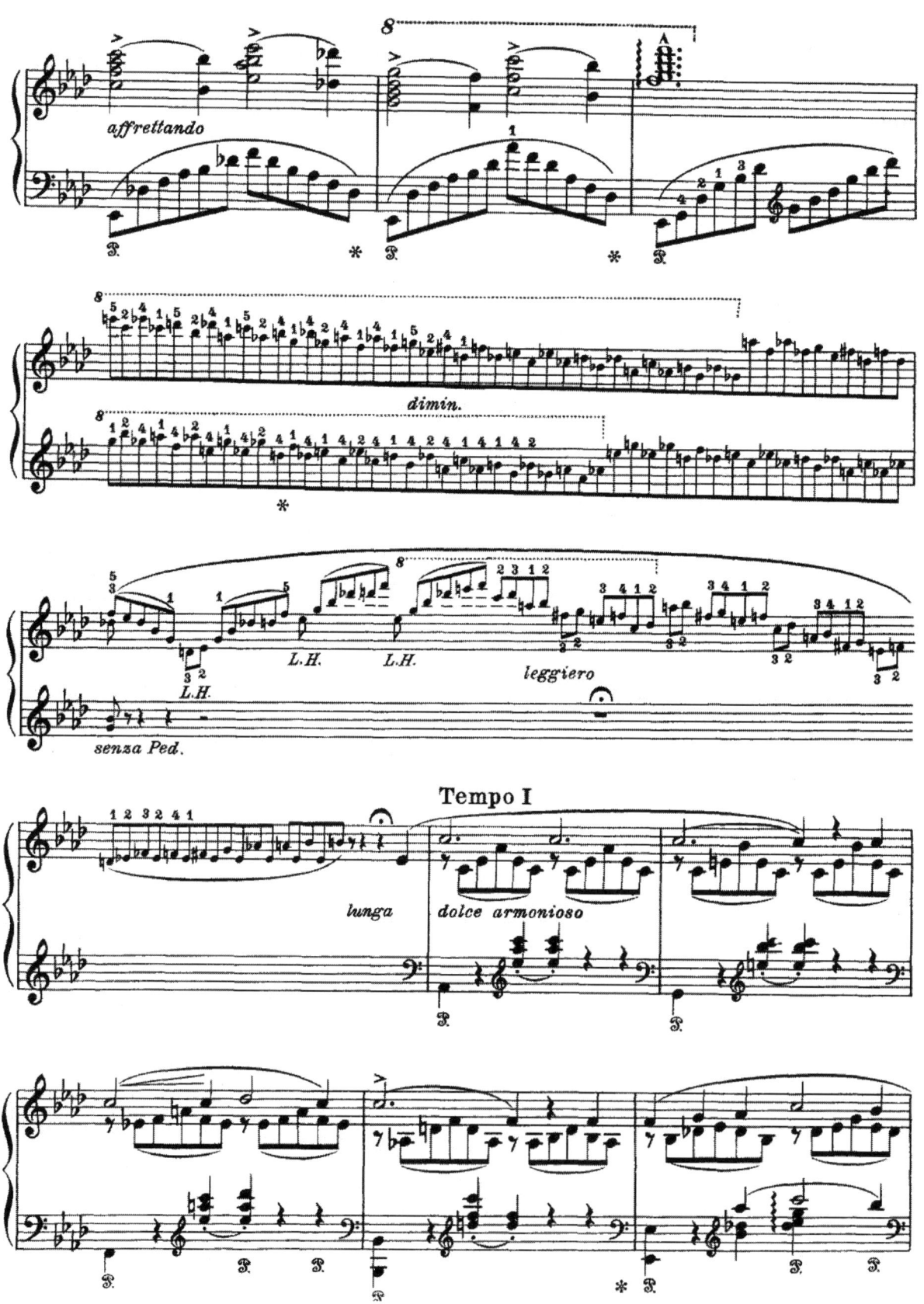

Sonatina in C Major (Op. 36- No. 1)

Rondeau

Là ci darem la mano

Nº 7. " Là ci darem la mano.,,
Duettino.

An - diam, an - diam, mio be - ne,___ a ri - sto-rar le pe - ne d'un'
With thee, with thee, my treasure,___ This life is naught but pleasure,___ My

An - diam, an - diam, mio be - ne, a ri - sto-rar le pe - ne d'un'
With thee, with thee, my treasure, This life is naught but pleasure, My

(Donna Elvira descends the steps, and

in - no - cen - te a - mor!
heart is___ fond - ly thine!

in - no - cen - te a - mor! An - diam!
heart is___ fond - ly thine! Oh come!

posts herself at centre, back.)

An - diam! An - diam!
I come! I'm thine!

An - Thou'rt

arco

An-diam, mio bene, an-diam, le pe-ne a ri - sto-rar d'un
My heart is fond - ly thine, my heart is fond - ly thine, my

diam! An-diam, mio bene, an-diam, le pe-ne a ri - sto-rar, d'un
mine! My heart is fond - ly thine, my heart is fond - ly thine, my

in - no - cen - te a - mor!
heart is fond - ly thine! (Exeunt, arm in arm.)

in - no - cen - te a - mor!
heart is fond - ly thine!

Recit.

Donna Elvira (desperately, intercepting Don Giovanni.)

Fer - ma - ti, scel - le - ra - to! il ciel mi fe - ce u - dir le tue per -
Leave her, thou vile se - du - cer! By heav'n I'm sent, thy per - fi - dy to

fi - die; io so - no a tem - po di sal - var que - ste mi - se - ra in - no -
wit - ness, and to pre - vent thee from de - lud - ing this poor girl's in - ex -

cen - te dal tuo bar - ba - ro ar - ti - glio! Me - schi - na! co - sa
pe - rience with thy treach - er - ous lan - guage! I won - der, says she

Zerlina.

Don Giovanni. (aside.) (softly to Elvira.)

sen - to! (Amor, con - si - glio!) I - dol mio, non ve - de - te, ch'io vo - glio di - ver -
tru - ly! (Cupid inspire me!) Can you chide, dear El - vi - ra, a lit - tle harmless

Donna Elvira (aloud.)

tir - mi? Di - ver - tir - ti? è ve - ro! di - ver - tir - ti! io sò, cru -
pas - time? Harmless pas - time? In - deed, Sir! harmless pas - time! De - ceit - ful

For Unto Us a Child is Born

For unto Us a Child is Born

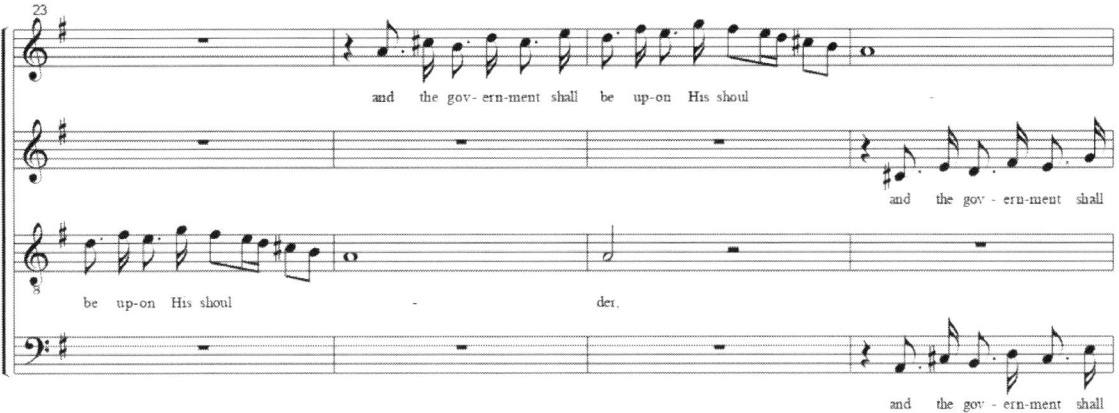

Won - der - ful   Coun - sel - lor,   The Might - y God,   The ev - er - last - ing Fa - ther,   Prince   of Peace!

Won - der - ful   Coun - sel - lor,   The Might - y God,   The ev - er - last - ing Fa - ther,   Prince   of Peace!

Won - der - ful   Coun - sel - lor,   The Might - y God,   The ev - er - last - ing Fa - ther,   Prince   of Peace!

Won - der - ful   Coun - sel - lor,   The Might - y God,   The ev - er - last - ing Fa - ther,   Prince   of Peace! Un - to

For un - to us a Child is born,

For un - to us a Child is born,

For un - to us a Child is born, un - to us   a Son is giv - en,   un - to

us a Child is born, un - to us a Child is born, un - to us   a Son is giv - en,   un - to

un - to us   a Son is giv - en, and the gov - ern - ment, the gov - ern - ment shall

un - to us   a Son is giv - en,   and the gov - ern - ment shall

us,   a Son   is   giv - en, un - to us   a Son is giv - en.

us,   a Son   is   giv - en, un - to us   a Son is giv - en.

hall Of The Mountain King By Grieg

178

Piano Learning Tips

Without learning to read the different notes on the treble and bass staff, you won't be able to play sheet music (the grand staff). To learn the notes on the staff, get a beginner's method book and this entertaining software, and practice it every day. Learning to read music requires a lot of time, struggle, and effort, but it is very worthwhile!

Regularly practice arpeggios, chords, and scales.

Scales, chords, and arpeggios will not only warm up your fingers at the beginning of your practice session, but they will also teach you some fundamental music theory, help you develop your technique, and strengthen your fingers. Start with C major Penta-scales, first with your hands apart, then with your hands together if you are a complete beginner. Once you've mastered that, try studying the parallel and contrarian motions of the C major scale. Triads and arpeggios can be added after learning a new key signature have been mastered.

Regularly practice sight reading.

Without any preparation or experience, sight reading is the process of reading and playing a song that you have never played before. Purchase a specialized book for sight reading, or just play a song that is a few levels below your present proficiency level. Sight reading will speed up the process of learning new music by putting your understanding of music theory and note-reading to the test.

Engage in everyday ear training.

Learn to recognize chords and intervals by ear. Play easy songs and clap back beats. Your piano training will benefit you immensely by developing your musical ear. (The Royal Conservatory of Music's online ear training is my preferred method of ear training practice. It is available at all levels, from absolute beginner to experienced, and the activities make everyday practice quick and simple!)

Acquire a foundational understanding of music theory.

Even if you don't have to be a music theory expert, having a basic understanding of the subject will improve your playing and your learning process. Learning to play the piano is similar to learning a new language, and studying music theory is similar to studying the syntax and rules of that language.

Sit straight-backed.

It will be challenging and uncomfortable to play the piano if you're slouching or sitting too near to it. Ensure that the bench is far enough back so that you can stand up easily between the bench and the piano, that your forearms are level with the keyboard, and that you are seated on the front half of the bench.

When learning a song, go through the notes, fingering, rhythms, emotion, and pace in that order.

Prior to learning the rhythms, make sure you are playing the correct notes with the appropriate fingering (don't forget any accidentals or sharps/flats specified by the key signature). Once you have a good understanding of these aspects, you can shape the melody by incorporating the expressive characteristics that the music specifies (crescendos/diminuendo, ritardando, staccato, sforzando, etc.). The music should then be sped up to match the performance tempo.

A song can be compared to a five-legged stool. The strength of the song is impacted when any one leg, such as the notes or rhythms, falters. You'll have a strong, beautifully played piece if you concentrate on the notes first, then work your way through the other "legs."

Employ the proper fingering.

It's difficult, time-consuming, and aggravating to play a piece with the wrong fingering. There will frequently be a suggested fingering printed in the sheet music, but this isn't always the case. Ask your piano instructor or view recordings of seasoned pianists performing the piece and use their fingering if you're unsure of what to do, as the foundation of music, scales, chords, and arpeggios are a great approach to really honing your finger technique.

Put the 3x3x3 rule into action.

Play hands together three times after practicing the right and left hands separately, three times each. With this straightforward technique, you can practice the individual components a lot before assembling them.

Put precision above speed.

No matter how skilled you are as a pianist, playing the appropriate notes always takes precedence over speeding through a piece. Fast, sloppy playing does not impress anyone; people like to hear an accurate performance at a slower tempo.

Many times, after learning a new set of measures rapidly, I assumed they were fine, only to discover that I was having trouble grasping the notes and rhythms. The incorrect way of learning is considerably more difficult to "un-learn" than the right way to learn something. When learning a piece, begin slowly and build up to the desired speed over time.

Keep the tempo steady.

When an instructor uses a metronome, many pupils will squirm. However, using a metronome is essential to playing at a constant speed. For performances, many songs will advise a metronome tempo; however, you should always begin learning a song at half speed.

Faqs

How long it takes a particular learner to "become good" at playing the piano?

It might depend on a variety of things. How much time do you spend practicing, for instance? Your progress will be significantly slowed down if you don't put in at least a half-hour to an hour each day.

Do you find yourself getting frustrated or bored if you play the piano for at least this long every day?

Breaking up your regular practice sessions into smaller, more manageable chunks might be the solution. If you practice the piano for at least this long every day, do you ever become discouraged or bored? The answer might be to divide up your usual practice periods into smaller, more manageable chunks.

What if you only want to play for entertainment or your own pleasure?

You might come up with a completely new idea of what it really means to be a good pianist as a result of this. You may begin to notice some significant and rewarding gains two to three years after beginning your classes, and this can make you very happy. However, you still have decades of study and training ahead of you if becoming a well-known concert pianist is your objective.

Do I need a piano teacher?

Before starting lessons, a lot of people have this question. After all, there are several online video tutorials and even books about self-teaching piano. These tools aren't necessarily bad, but it's always a great idea to work with a qualified and experienced teacher at some time, especially if you want to advance your piano playing beyond just for fun.

Although it is not necessary to have a tutor if a student only sometimes wants to sit down and play their favorite songs on the piano, there is no substitute for the advice and insight that a good teacher can offer. Formal lessons are unquestionably the best point to start whether you want to play professionally.

How do I choose the best piano instructor?

Too many beginning pianists just choose the first teacher they come across. This is okay in some cases, but it often pays to check around a little before selecting the best instructor for you or your child.

In terms of their personal training, the majority of piano instructors most likely possess admirable backgrounds and are totally qualified. This does not imply that every instructor is equally qualified to instruct you or your child, though. Each teacher has their own distinct style. Some pupils could be drawn to this style, while others might not.

It can be really challenging to choose the "ideal" piano teacher for your child if they have never taken piano lessons before. The unsuitable teacher can make learning the piano frustrating and heartbreaking since the student won't pick it up and won't be motivated by a passion for playing the piano.

It makes sense to request short audition lessons from a variety of teachers for this reason. To give your child a chance to interact with each instructor for about 30 minutes, try to schedule these with at least three instructors. Ask your youngster how each instructor made him feel. Was the lesson fun to learn? Would he prefer to meet with this instructor each week? Pick the caregiver who seems to connect with your child the best. You can always switch to a different instructor later if it turns out to be a mistake.

Do I need to learn music theory?

Both adult and young pupils may find learning to read music to be a challenging task. Is it truly necessary? It may not be because they are particularly talented at playing by ear for certain students.

Even if you find that you are quite proficient at playing by ear, learning how to read music is by far the superior course of action. Knowing how to read music gives you a dependable, standardized approach to comprehending music and how it ought to be played and sounded. Learning to read is quite similar to learning to read music. Instead of having someone else read, it is more practical for each person to learn to read the words on their own. Instead of having someone else read aloud while the listener tries to memorize all the words in the story, it is more practical for each person to learn to read the words themselves.

It can be scary to learn to read music, but it doesn't have to be. Anyone who is motivated to learn can master the art of reading music. You can continue your study by using internet tools, flashcards, and other materials in addition to the assistance your piano teacher will undoubtedly provide. Don't let your fear keep you from learning to read music because it can be the key to improving your piano skills.

What age is ideal for learning the piano?

It would be lovely to suggest that there is a magic age when piano lessons should start, but the truth is much more nuanced. At the age of three or four, some kids are natural pianists, but students as old as 70 have also performed admirably. The "ideal age" to learn to play the piano is a myth. Really, all that is required is the willingness to put in the effort and the desire to pursue it.

What exactly are piano lessons teaching?

Every lesson has the potential to cover a wide range of topics. Here are some examples of subjects that might be studied in a piano class:

- Aural training
- Rhythmic drills
- Reading music is a skill.
- Effective practice methods
- A good playing style
- Stance and holding of the hands

There are a virtually limitless number of ways to teach these diverse courses. Some of these are based on the student's age. For instance, many young piano students are taught through games and riddles, and for older students, playing various exercises and songs can explain musical principles.

Is musical talent a requirement?

Do you consider yourself to be tone-deaf? Has no one in your family ever studied singing or an instrument? Nevertheless, playing the piano is something that you or your child is interested in learning. That is totally okay. You don't need to have any prior knowledge, expertise, or talent to attend your first piano lesson. If you tell your teacher that you have never studied music, she will create an introductory program to assist you in understanding a topic that may seem like a foreign language to you. When something doesn't seem to be working out, be sure to investigate why and make a commitment to daily practice. You'll soon begin to hone musical skills you never realized you possessed.

Final Notes

Are you ready to play your piano and keyboard? Well, even after learning everything about a piano and its keys, you won't be able to play it like a pro, and only practice will help you play even the toughest of the rhymes on your keyboard. So go ahead, practice slowly and learn different chords to play on your own, then start practicing the given melodies!

Made in the USA
Middletown, DE
20 April 2023

29164671R00104